Sage Sayings:
Inspiring Native American Passages for Leaders

Compiled by

JOHN & JOANN GIRARD

This work is licensed under the Creative Commons Attribution 4.0 International License.
To view a copy of this license, visit http://creativecommons.org/licenses/by/4.0/

You are free to:
- **Share** — copy and redistribute the material in any medium or format
- **Adapt** — remix, transform, and build upon the material
- for any purpose, even commercially.

The licensor cannot revoke these freedoms as long as you follow the license terms.

Under the following terms:
- **Attribution** — You must give **appropriate credit**, provide a link to the license, and **indicate if changes were made**. You may do so in any reasonable manner, but not in any way that suggests the licensor endorses you or your use.
- **No additional restrictions** — You may not apply legal terms or **technological measures** that legally restrict others from doing anything the license permits.

2014, John & JoAnn Girard

ISBN: 978-1497432048
ISBN-10: 1497432049

Cover Photo: Theodore Roosevelt National Park, John Girard

DEDICATION

To Sara and Cynthia,
Our next generation of leaders

CONTENTS

Acknowledgments   i

Sage Sayings   1

About the People   87

About the Authors   115

Index   117

ACKNOWLEDGMENTS

The inspiration for this book comes from our friend Dr. Madanmohan Rao who introduced us to the power of proverbs through this book *Pearls of Wisdom: Indian Proverbs & Quotations*.

SAGE SAYINGS

The pages that follow include some of the most inspiring, thought provoking, and sagacious words we have ever read. We certainly take no credit in penning these *sage sayings* nor can we, with much certainty, guarantee their authenticity. Nevertheless, the works that follow, we are very certain, will cause you to pause, reflect, and perhaps even reprioritize.

The collection includes proverbs, prayers, and quotations that we believe were written or spoken by a group of very wise men and women. As far as we can determine the origin of each of these seminal passages was a Native American. We use this term with the greatest respect and understand that many people prefer different collective nouns for the diverse group of people. In our home country, Canada, many people prefer the term First Nations whereas in our adopted country, the United States, the term Native American seems more common. We ask that you think beyond the label and consider the incredible wisdom contained in the words.

The sayings are presented in an unsystematic manner - there really is no rhyme or reason for the order. We hope this enhances your discovery of the passages. For many, the best way to enjoy the book will be to open it to a random page and start reading. Of course, some may prefer to read it cover-to-cover and that is just fine as well. For those looking for a particular theme or word we have added an index to make your quest a little easier.

As interesting as we find the quotes, proverbs, and prayers - *the sage sayings* - perhaps the most fascinating exploration is the people behind the words. As we read their works we cannot help but notice their common sense, connection to the planet, and recognition of family. These important ideas seem to be lost in many of the decisions that are made in our 24/7 ever-connected world in which so many of us live and work. We wonder if the next generations of readers will think we were as wise.

Following the Sage Sayings we have included a very brief overview of the people responsible for the words of wisdom. We hope this concise description will spark your interest to conduct your own research about these amazing people.

We have tried very hard to make sure we accurately acknowledge the true author of the words. Equally we have worked diligently to ensure that most accurate translation or transcription is used. In both cases we are certain there will be errors. There may be some debate about the correct clan of the author(s). Again we have done our best to list the most up to date term being used, but we would appreciate you suggesting corrections. In some cases, especially where there is contradictory evidence, we simply list the source as *unknown*. This compilation includes about 500 sayings we discovered. We know there are many more worthy of reading and we welcome suggested additions. Please help us make the collection more accurate by contacting us with any information that you have about our errors, omissions, or misrepresentations.

We hope you enjoy our compilation.

> John & JoAnn Girard
> john@sagesayings.info
> joann@sagesayings.info
> www.sagesayings.info

SAGE SAYINGS

Knowledge is rooted in all things — the world is a library.

~ Lakota Proverb

Never say that you really want to see an animal. You may see one too close for comfort.

~ Inuit Proverb

The good looking boy may be just good in the face.

~ Apache Proverb

All around me my land is beauty.

~ Navajo Proverb

When the last tree has been cut down, the last fish caught, the last river poisoned, only then will we realize that one cannot eat money.

~ Alanis Obomsawin, Abenaki

Strive to be a person who is never absent from an important act.

~ Osage Proverb

Do not judge your neighbor until you walk two moons in his moccasins.

> **~ Cheyenne Proverb**

There is one God looking down on us all.

> **~ Geronimo, Chiracahua Apache**

All of Creation is related.

> **~ White Buffalo Calf Woman, Lakota**

Do not speak of evil for it creates curiosity in the hearts of the young.

> **~ Lakota Proverb**

All men were made by the Great Spirit Chief. They are all brothers.

> **~ Chief Joseph, Nez Perce**

When you die, you will be spoken of as those in the sky, like the stars.

> **~ Yurok Proverb**

When the Earth is sick, the animals will begin to disappear, when that happens, The Warriors of the Rainbow will come to save them.

~ Chief Seattle, Duwamish

The strong man walks with virtue.

~ Zuni Proverb

Don't be afraid to cry. It will free your mind of sorrowful thoughts.

~ Hopi Proverb

It makes no difference as to the name of the God, since love is the real God of all the world.

~ Apache Proverb

It is my wish and the wishes of my people to live peaceably and quietly with you.

~ Cornplanter, Seneca Chief

Old age is not as honorable as death, but most people want it.

~ Crow Proverb

The earth and myself are of one mind.

> ~ **Chief Joseph, Nez Perce**

The rain falls on the just and the unjust.

> ~ **Hopi Proverb**

Inner peace and love are God's greatest gifts.

> ~ **Sioux Proverb**

The life of a man is a circle from childhood to childhood.

> ~ **Black Elk, Oglala Lakota**

I believe much trouble and blood would be saved if we opened our hearts more.

> ~ **Chief Joseph, Nez Perce**

We always return to our first loves.

> ~ **Unknown**

There is a way out of every dark mist; over a rainbow trail.

> ~ **Navajo Proverb**

Follow my footprints.

> **~ Inuit Proverb**

There are many good moccasin tracks along the trail of a straight arrow.

> **~ Sioux Proverb**

Don't be afraid to weep—it will free your mind from sad thoughts.

> **~ Hopi Proverb**

Be satisfied with the needs instead of the wants.

> **~ Sioux Proverb**

Each soul must meet the morning sun, the new sweet earth, and the Great Silence alone!

> **~ Charles Eastman, Lakota**

We do not want churches because they will teach us to quarrel about God.

> **~ Chief Joseph, Nez Perce**

Everything has form, power, and inner meaning.

> ~ **Hopi Proverb**

All things share the same breath — the beast, the tree, the man, the air shares its spirit with all the life it supports.

> ~ **Chief Seattle, Duwamish**

Tell me, and I will listen. Show me, and I will understand. Involve me, and I will learn.

> ~ **Lakota Proverb**

Let us see—is this real, this life that I am living?

> ~ **Pawnee Proverb**

With all things and in all things, we are relatives.

> ~ **Sioux Proverb**

Our Creator put us here on earth. He gave us different languages to use. He put us here to love and respect each other.

> ~ **John Mosquito, Nekaneet**

Let us all be meat, to nourish one another, that we all may grow."

~ **Cheyenne Proverb**

We give back thanks to our mother, the earth that sustains us.

~ **Onondaga Proverb**

It takes a whole village to raise a child.

~ **Omaha Proverb**

The more you ask how far you need to go, the longer your journey seems.

~ **Seneca Proverb**

When a man moves away from nature his heart becomes hard.

~ **Lakota Proverb**

Not every sweet root gives birth to sweet grass.

~ **Anishinabe Proverb**

The soul would have no rainbow if the eyes had no tears.

~ **Minquass Proverb**

Listen to the whispers and you won't have to hear the screams.

~ **Cherokee Proverb**

The time for the lone wolf is over.

~ **Hopi Proverb**

As long as you live, keep learning how to live.

~ **Seneca Proverb**

Always treat children with respect; they will replace you one day.

~ **Inuit Proverb**

When the white man discovered this country, Indians were running it. No taxes, no debt, women did all the work. White man thought he could improve on a system like this.

~ **Cherokee Proverb**

That hand is not the color of your hand. ... The Great Spirit made us both.

~ Standing Bear, Ponca

The love of possessions is a weakness to be overcome.

~ Santee Proverb

You can't get rich if you look after your relatives properly.

~ Navajo Proverb

How smooth must be the language of the whites, when they can make right look like wrong, and wrong like right.

~ Black Hawk, Sauk

Let us walk softly on the Earth with all living beings great and small.

~ Cherokee Proverb

Seek wisdom, not knowledge. Knowledge is of the past, wisdom is of the future.

~ Lumbee Proverb

There is a need for obedience all around us.

~ **Sauk Proverb**

Even a small mouse has anger.

~ **Unknown**

It is better to return a borrowed pot with a little something you last cooked in it.

~ **Omaha Proverb**

Tenskwatawa has never spoken a lie or an impurity, and never will.

~ **Tenskwatawa, Shawnee**

Don't judge a person until you've walked two moons in his moccasins.

~ **Cheyenne Proverb**

Those who live for one another learn that love is the bond of perfect unity.

~ **Fools Crow, Lakota spiritual leader**

An Indian leader is a servant of the people.

~ Scott Momaday, Kiowa

In an eagle there is all the wisdom of the world.

~ Lame Deer, Minnicoujou

It is good to tell one's heart.

~ Chippewa Proverb

Listen, or your tongue will make you deaf.

~ Unknown

Ask questions from your heart, and you will receive answers from your heart.

~ Omaha Proverb

When a fox walks lame, the old rabbit jumps.

~ Unknown

People seeking a myth will usually find one.

~ Pueblo Proverb

Prepare a noble death song for the day when you go over the great divide.

~ Chief Tecumseh, Shawnee

There is a right time and place for everything.

~ Cherokee Proverb

The elders say, 'The longest road you're going to have to walk is from here to here. From your head to your heart.' But they also say you can't speak to the people as a leader unless you've made the return journey. From the heart back to the head.

~ Dakota Proverb

Everything the power does, it does in a circle.

~ Lakota Proverb

Let go of the shore.

~ Hopi Proverb

My friend, I am old but I shall never die. I shall always love in my children, and children's children.

~ New Corn, Potawatomi chief

If you wear the same clothes that you use in town to go hunting, they will be very cold.

~ Inuit Proverb

Although we are in different boats, you in your boat and we in our canoe, we share the same river of life.

~ Chief Oren Lyons, Onandaga

You have to check the weather the minute that you get up.

~ Inuit Proverb

Anyone who is willing to live the life I have led can do the things I do.

~ Fools Crow, Lakota spiritual leader

Be good to each other.

~ Hopi Proverb

The only things that need the protection of men are the things of men, not the things of the spirit.

~ Crow Proverb

Our first teacher is our own heart.

~ **Cheyenne Proverb**

Lose your temper and you lose a friend; lie and you lose yourself.

~ **Hopi Proverb**

You can't wake a person who is pretending to be asleep.

~ **Navajo Proverb**

Beauty is before me, And beauty is behind me. Above and below me hovers the beautiful. I am surrounded by it. I am immersed in it. In my youth I am aware of it, And in old age I shall walk quietly The beautiful trail.

~ **Navajo Prayer**

All dreams spin out from the same web.

~ **Hopi Proverb**

The growing and dying of the moon reminds us of our ignorance which comes and goes — but when the moon is full it is as if the Great Spirit were upon the whole world.

~ **Black Elk, Oglala Lakota**

Pray to understand what man has forgotten.

~ Lumbee Proverb

Good and evil cannot dwell together in the same heart, so a good man ought not go into evil company.

~ Delaware Proverb

It may be that one little root of the sacred tree still lives. Nourish it, then, that it may leaf and bloom; and fill with singing birds.

~ Chippewa Proverb

The man who preserves his selfhood is ever calm and unshaken by the storms of existence.

~ Charles Eastman, Dakota

Sharing and giving are the ways of God.

~ Sauk Proverb

What is past is past — it is the present and the future that concern us.

~ Hiawatha, Onondaga and Mohawk

To watch us dance is to hear our hearts speak.

~ **Derrick "Suwaima" Davis, Hopi/Chocktaw**

The world is a library and its books are the stones, leaves, grass, brooks, birds, and animals.

~ **Chief Luther Standing Bear, Oglala Lakota**

When all the trees have been cut down, when all the animals have been hunted, when all the waters are polluted, when all the air is unsafe to breathe, only then will you discover you cannot eat money.

~ **Cree Proverb**

Do not allow yesterday to spend up too much of today.

~ **Cherokee Proverb**

A nation is not conquered until the hearts of its women are on the ground. Then it is finished, no matter how brave its warriors or how strong their weapons.

~ **Lakota Proverb**

It is easy to be brave from a safe distance.

~ **Omaha Proverb**

Give thanks for unknown blessings already on their way.

~ Unknown

Everything the power does, it does in a circle.

~ Lakota Proverb

Life is both giving and receiving.

~ Mohawk Proverb

Work hard, keep the ceremonies, live peaceably, and unite your hearts.

~ Hopi Proverb

I want no blood upon my land to stain the grass. I want it all clear and pure, and I wish it so, that all who go through among my people may find peace when they come in, and leave it when they go out.

~ Ten Bears of the Yapparika Comanche

Flowers do not force their way with great strife. Flowers open to perfection slowly in the sun.

~ White Eagle, Ponca

One does not sell the land people walk on.

> **~ Crazy Horse, Oglala Lakota**

Talk was given to the people for good.

> **~ Sauk Proverb**

Is it not better for one hundred to pray for one than for one to pray alone for himself?

> **~ Sioux Proverb**

Treachery darkens the chain of friendship, but truth makes it brighter than ever.

> **~ Conestoga Proverb**

All things share the same breath—the animal, the tree, the man, and the air shares its spirit with all the life it supports.

> **~ Chief Seattle, Duwamish**

The bird who has eaten cannot fly with the bird that is hungry.

> **~ Omaha Proverb**

The weakness of the enemy makes our strength.

~ Cherokee Proverb

We are going by you without fighting if you will let us, but we are going by you anyhow.

~ Chief Joseph, Nez Perce

Listen to nature's voice—it contains treasures for you.

~ Huron Proverb

Children are taught to give what they prize most, that they may taste the happiness of giving.

~ Santee Proverb

We give thanks back to the Sun that has looked upon the Earth with beneficial eyes.

~ Onondaga Proverb

Service is the rent we pay for living, the anchor to our humanity.

~ Oneida Proverb

All people cry; some just don't show it.

~ Inuit Proverb

Man has responsibility, not power.

~ Tuscarora Proverb

Don't let the grass grow on the path of friendship.

~ Blackfoot Proverb

After dark all cats are leopards.

~ Zuni Proverb

Words are the voice of the heart.

~ Tuscarora Proverb

If a man loses anything and goes back and looks carefully for it, he will find it.

~ Chief Sitting Bull, Lakota

Show respect for all men, but grovel to none.

~ Shawnee Proverb

Distribute your catch evenly with all the hunting party.

~ Inuit Proverb

Don't eat snow when you are thirsty. Snow is your best friend.

~ Inuit Proverb

The Earth is the mother of everyone, and everyone should have equal rights upon it.

~ Chief Joseph, Nez Perce

You must live your life from beginning to end. No one else can do it for you.

~ Hopi Proverb

To go on a vision quest is to go into the presence of the great mystery.

~ Lakota Proverb

Don't sing or talk while you eat.

~ Inuit Proverb

Tell me and I'll forget. Show me, and I may not remember. Involve me, and I'll understand.

~ Unknown

You must always be careful with something that is greater than you are.

~ Shoshone Proverb

The Northern lights will take your head off and play soccer with it, if you whistle at them, or stay out too late.

~ Inuit Proverb

Family is what keeps us happy! Being together, helping one another out is what family is all about.

~ Vital Daniels, Sturgeon Lake First Nation

White men have too many chiefs.

~ Nez Perce Proverb

We do not want riches. We want peace and love.

~ Red Cloud, Oglala Lakota

See how the boy is with his sister and you can know how the man will be with his daughter.

~ Plains Proverb

The man who freely gives his opinion should be ready to fight fiercely.

~ Iowa Proverb

We are friends; we must assist each other to bear our burdens.

~ Osage Proverb

Everything on the earth has a purpose, every disease an herb to cure it, and every person a mission. This is the Indian theory of existence.

~ Mourning Dove

You can't purchase friendship—you have to do your part to make it.

~ Sauk Proverb

How smooth must be the language of the whites, when they can make right look like wrong, and wrong like right.

~ Black Hawk, Sauk

I was warmed by the sun, rocked by the winds and sheltered by the trees as other Indian babes. I can go everywhere with a good feeling.

~ Geronimo, Chiracahua Apache

Your dogs should be raised like the way you raise children.

~ Inuit Proverb

If you see no reason for giving thanks, the fault lies in yourself.

~ Minquass Proverb

To be noble is to give to those who have less. It is an issue of service and leadership.

~ Oneida Proverb

Inside your heart is a tiny place where all knowledge and wisdom resides.

~ Hopi Proverb

Do things quickly, don't delay when you are asked to do something. Otherwise, your (wife, future wife) will have a lengthy hard labor.

~ Inuit Proverb

I have been to the end of the earth, I have been to the end of the waters, I have been to the end of the sky, I have been to the end of the mountains, I have found none that are not my friends.

~ Navajo Proverb

Be truthful and respectful in our speech, which in itself is a miracle and a gift from the Creator, that we might use it only to speak good of each other and pass on the good things of life.

~ Cree Proverb

Whatever we do affects everything in the universe.

~ White Buffalo Calf Woman, Lakota

Judge not by the eye but by the heart.

~ Cheyenne Proverb

In age, talk; in childhood, tears.

~ Hopi Proverb

Seek to make your life long and its purpose in the service of your people.

~ Chief Tecumseh, Shawnee

A rocky vineyard does not need a prayer, but a pick ax.

~ **Navajo Proverb**

Whatever you need on all levels of your existence is there for you.

~ **Hopi Proverb**

Before leaving your host, give him a little present—it will serve as a little courtesy, and will not offend.

~ **Seneca Proverb**

Do not wrong or hate your neighbor for it is not he that you wrong but yourself.

~ **Pima Proverb**

Knowing your language gives you an inner strength and pride in your heritage.

~ **Freda Ahenakew, Muskeg Lake First Nation**

Speak truth in humility to all people. Only then can you be a true man.

~ **Sioux Proverb**

Life is not independent from death—it only appears that way.

~ **Blackfoot Proverb**

We see no need for a setting apart one day in seven as a holy day, because to us all days are God's days.

~ **Sioux Proverb**

Those that lie down with dogs, get up with fleas.

~ **Blackfoot Proverb**

Let your eyes be offended by the sight of lying and deceitful men.

~ **Hopi Proverb**

Service is a spiritual act.

~ **Oneida Proverb**

The Great Spirit is in all things, he is in the air we breathe. The Great Spirit is our Father, but the Earth is our Mother. She nourishes us, that which we put into the ground she returns to us.

~ **Big Thunder, Abenaki**

Where no one intrudes, many can live in harmony.

> **~ Chief Dan George, Tsleil-Waututh**

Don't let yesterday use up too much of today.

> **~ Cherokee Proverb**

The parents are the ones who should teach the young about the language, the culture and the traditional worldview.

> **~ Helen Fineday, Sweetgrass First Nation**

I see the universe; I see myself.

> **~ High Eagle, Cherokee**

When we show our respect for other living things, they respond with respect for us.

> **~ Arapaho Proverb**

Being Indian is mainly in your heart. It's a way of walking with the earth instead of upon it.

> **~ David Ipinia, Yurok**

Let us put our minds together and see what future we can make for our children.

~ **Chief Joseph, Nez Perce**

The coward shoots with shut eyes.

~ **Unknown**

O' Great Spirit, help me always to speak the truth quietly, to listen with an open mind when others speak, and to remember the peace that may be found in silence.

~ **Cherokee Prayer**

To touch the earth is to have harmony with nature.

~ **Lakota Proverb**

No one else can represent your conscience.

~ **Anishinabe Proverb**

The ground on which we stand is sacred ground. It is the blood of our ancestors.

~ **Aleek-chea-ahoosh, Crow chief**

Too many misinterpretations have been made ... too many misunderstandings.

~ **Chief Joseph, Nez Perce**

He who has great power should use it lightly.

~ **Seneca Proverb**

If you want to see what your body will look like tomorrow, look at your thoughts today.

~ **Navajo Proverb**

Life's greatest danger lies in the fact that man's food consists entirely of souls.

~ **Inuit Proverb**

Our hearts stay young if we let them.

~ **Pretty Shield, Crow**

Never get involved in someone's decisions about his belongings.

~ **Hopi Proverb**

We are all one, brothers.

~ Hopi Proverb

Treat the earth well: it was not given to you by your parents, it was loaned to you by your children. We do not inherit the Earth from our Ancestors, we borrow it from our Children.

~ Unknown

We are all one child spinning through Mother Sky.

~ Shawnee Proverb

Man's law changes with his understanding of man. Only the laws of the spirit remain always the same.

~ Crow Proverb

Live your life that the fear of death can never enter your heart.

~ Chief Tecumseh, Shawnee

If you swallow caribou hair while eating, you will get an itchy ass.

~ Inuit Proverb

're nothing good to say, don't say anything at all.

> ~ **Inuit Proverb**

All plants are our siblings. If we listen, we can hear them speaking.

> ~ **Arapaho Proverb**

The way of the troublemaker is thorny.

> ~ **Umpqua Proverb**

Treat your grandchildren like your own children.

> ~ **Inuit Proverb**

Be still and the earth will speak to you.

> ~ **Navajo Proverb**

Wakan Tanka, Great Mystery, teach me how to trust my heart, my mind, my intuition, my inner knowing, the senses of my body, the blessings of my spirit. Teach me to trust these things so that I may enter my Sacred Space and love beyond my fear, and thus Walk in Balance with the passing of each glorious Sun.

> ~ **Lakota Prayer**

There can never be peace between nations until it is first known that true peace is within the souls of men.

~ Sioux Proverb

All we wanted was peace and to be let alone.

~ Crazy Horse, Oglala Lakota

Eternal life without suffering was yours all along. Never were you ever separated from the Source.

~ Hopi Proverb

Misfortunes do not flourish on one path, they grow everywhere.

~ Pawnee Proverb

I have been shown how to open the door that has shut us out from joy.

~ Tenskwatawa, Shawnee

Healthy feet can hear the very heart of holy Earth.

~ Chief Sitting Bull, Lakota

Make my enemy brave and strong, so that if defeated, I will not be ashamed.

~ Plains Proverb

Be self-loving—go outside yourself and take action. Be peaceful, and be focused on the solution.

~ Sioux Proverb

Before me peaceful, behind me peaceful, under me peaceful, over me peaceful, all around me peaceful.

~ Navajo Proverb

Great men are usually destroyed by those who are jealous of them.

~ Sioux Proverb

The frog does not drink up the pond in which he lives.

~ Sioux Proverb

Animals are more abundant after a storm or a blizzard.

~ Inuit Proverb

Remember that your children are not your own, but are lent to you by the Creator.

~ Mohawk Proverb

The more you give, the more good things come to you.

~ Crow Proverb

God gives us each a song.

~ Ute Proverb

It does not require many words to speak the truth.

~ Chief Joseph, Nez Perce

Many have fallen with the bottle in their hand.

~ Lakota Proverb

Creation is ongoing.

~ Lakota Proverb

It is easy to be brave from a distance.

~ Omaha Proverb

The true Indian's generosity is limited only by strength and ability.

> ~ **Sioux Proverb**

Always remember that a smile is something sacred, to be shared.

> ~ **Cherokee Proverb**

We must relearn how to cry. A strong man cries; it is the weak man who holds back his tears.

> ~ **Lame Deer, Lakota**

You are a servant of the people and the people must come first.

> ~ **Norbert Hill, Oneida**

Take your children where you go — and don't be ashamed.

> ~ **Hopi Proverb**

The greatest strength is gentleness.

> ~ **Iroquois Proverb**

SAGE SAYINGS

You can't wake a person who is pretending to be asleep.

~ Navajo Proverb

Prestige is accorded those who give unreservedly.

~ Sioux Proverb

Silence is the cornerstone of character.

~ Charles Eastman, Dakota

We are grateful to the Mother Earth.

~ Pueblo Proverb

Know the river has its destination.

~ Hopi Proverb

All religions are but stepping stones back to God.

~ Pawnee Proverb

Our first teacher is our own heart.

~ Cheyenne Proverb

I salute the light within your eyes where the whole Universe dwells. For when you are at the centre within yourself, and I within mine, we shall be as one.

> ~ **Crazy Horse, Oglala Lakota**

Children must early learn the beauty of generosity.

> ~ **Santee Proverb**

I add my breath to your breath that we shall be as one people.

> ~ **Pueblo Proverb**

What is past and cannot be prevented should not be grieved for.

> ~ **Pawnee Proverb**

Before eating, always take time to thank the food.

> ~ **Arapaho Proverb**

There are many ways to God.

> ~ **Arapaho Proverb**

May the Warm Winds of Heaven, Blow softly upon your house. May the Great Spirit, Bless all who enter there. May your Mocassins, Make happy tracks in many snows, and may the Rainbow Always touch your shoulder.

> **~ Cherokee Prayer**

A good chief gives, he does not take.

> **~ Mohawk Proverb**

When you are at that center within you and I am that place within me, we shall be one.

> **~ Crazy Horse, Oglala Lakota**

Leave your mind and your constant thoughts and return to your heart.

> **~ Hopi Proverb**

Who serves his fellows is of all the greatest.

> **~ Dakota Proverb**

When an elder speaks, be silent and listen.

> **~ Mohawk Proverb**

There is never a valid reason for arguing.

~ **Hopi Proverb**

You already possess everything necessary to become great.

~ **Crow Proverb**

Nothing is more honorable than a grateful heart.

~ **Seneca Proverb**

Respect everyone, but lower yourself to no one.

~ **Shawnee Proverb**

A child believes that only the actions of someone who is unfriendly can cause pain.

~ **Santee Proverb**

Love one another and help one another.

~ **Cree Proverb**

Stand in the light when you want to speak out.

~ **Crow Proverb**

When you arise in the morning give thanks for the food and for the joy of living.

~ Chief Tecumseh, Shawnee

In our every deliberation, we must consider the impact of our decisions on the next 7 generations.

~ Iroquois Proverb

There are no secrets or mysteries—there is only common sense.

~ Onondaga Proverb

The laws of man change, but the laws of the spirit stay the same.

~ Crow Proverb

Some are smart but they are not wise.

~ Shoshone Proverb

You can get married when you can build an igloo.

~ Inuit Proverb

If two different bowls both get the job done, then what difference does it make if one bowl is dark and the other is pale?

> ~ **Hopi Proverb**

When you lose the rhythm of the drumbeat of God, you are lost from the peace and rhythm of life.

> ~ **Cheyenne Proverb**

It is the mothers, not the warriors, who create a people and guide their destiny.

> ~ **Chief Luther Standing Bear, Oglala Sioux**

When the grandmothers speak, the world will begin to heal.

> ~ **Hopi Proverb**

Remember who you really are, trust yourself, and open your eyes to the beauty of a new Earth unfolding before you as we breathe.

> ~ **Hopi Proverb**

A community that lacks faith in itself cannot survive.

> ~ **Hopi Proverb**

Guard your tongue in youth, and in age you may mature a thought that will be of service to your people.

~ Minquass Proverb

Never sit while your seniors stand.

~ Cree Proverb

No answer is also an answer.

~ Hopi Proverb

There are plenty of different paths to a deep understanding of the universe.

~ Blackfoot Proverb

Life is not separate from death. It only looks that way.

~ Blackfoot Proverb

Skin color makes no difference ... My skin is red, but my grandfather was a white man. But why should that matter? It is not the color of the skin that makes me good or bad.

~ Chief White Shield, Arikara

The true Indian regards it as an honor to be selected for a difficult or dangerous service.

> ~ **Sioux Proverb**

A good soldier is a poor scout.

> ~ **Cheyenne Proverb**

Take only memories, leave nothing but footprints.

> ~ **Chief Seattle, Duwamish**

All I want is right and just.

> ~ **Red Cloud, Oglala Lakota**

Regard Heaven as your father, Earth as your Mother and all things as your Brothers and Sisters.

> ~ **Unknown**

The Indians in their simplicity give away all they have — above all to the poor and the aged from whom they can hope for no return.

> ~ **Sioux Proverb**

Take only what you need and leave the land as you found it.

~ **Arapaho Proverb**

Never go to sleep when your meat is on the fire.

~ **Pueblo Proverb**

You cannot see the future with tears in your eyes.

~ **Navajo Proverb**

I am tired of talk that comes to nothing. It makes my heart sick when I remember all the good words and all the broken promises. There has been too much talking by men who had no right to talk.

~ **Chief Joseph, Nez Perce**

Never trouble anyone regarding his religion—respect him in his beliefs, and demand that he respect yours.

~ **Tecumseh, Shawnee**

There is beauty around me and there is beauty within me.

~ **Navajo Proverb**

I do not think the measure of a civilization is how tall its buildings of concrete are but rather how well its people have learned to relate to their environment and fellow man.

~ Sun Bear, Chippewa

When it comes time to die, be not like those whose hearts are filled with the fear of death, so when their time comes they weep and pray for a little more time to live their lives over again in a different way. Sing your death song, and die like a hero going home.

~ Chief Aupumut, Mohican

Listening to a liar is like drinking warm water.

~ Apache Proverb

If you want to learn your language you need to use it!!!

~ Freda Ahenakew, Muskeg Lake First Nation

We must protect the forests for our children, grandchildren and children yet to be born. We must protect the forests for those who can't speak for themselves such as the birds, animals, fish and trees.

~ Qwatsinas, Nuxalk First Nation

Like the spider we must return again to rebuild webs by bringing together threads of our lives — uniting them to divine center within.

~ Hopi Proverb

Once I was in Victoria, and I saw a very large house. They told me it was a bank and that the white men place their money there to be taken care of, and that by and by they got it back with interest. We are Indians and we have no such bank; but when we have plenty of money or blankets, we give them away to other chiefs and people, and by and by they return them with interest, and our hearts feel good. Our way of giving is our bank.

~ Chief Maquinna, Nootka

A smile explains everything.

~ Inuit Proverb

Respect the gift and the giver.

~ Omaha Proverb

If the white man wants to live in peace with the Indian, he can live in peace.

~ Chief Joseph, Nez Perce

Every fire is the same size when it starts.

> **~ Seneca Proverb**

Don't judge with the eyes—use the heart instead.

> **~ Cheyenne Proverb**

Dreams are wiser than men.

> **~ Omaha Proverb**

Every animal knows more than you do.

> **~ Nez Perce Proverb**

We are like birds with a broken wing.

> **~ Chief Plenty Coups, Crow**

A very great vision is needed and the man who has it must follow it as the eagle seeks the deepest blue of the sky.

> **~ Crazy Horse, Oglala Lakota**

Reading to oneself is boring; read to others and share.

> **~ Inuit Proverb**

You can get married when you can sew well.

~ Inuit Proverb

Beauty before me, with it I wander. Beauty behind me, with it I wander. Beauty below me, with it I wander. Beauty above me, with it I wander.

~ Navajo Prayer

There is no death, only a change of worlds.

~ Duwamish Proverb

Be humble.

~ Hopi Proverb

Never let things slide: keep steady hold, each upon yourself — do not throw away your life simply to spite another.

~ Cree Proverb

True leadership is only possible when character is more important than authority.

~ Joseph Marshall, Lakota

Beware of the man who does not talk, and the dog that does not bark.

~ **Cheyenne Proverb**

You look at me and you see only an ugly old man, but within I am filled with great beauty.

~ **Old Man Buffalo Grass, Navajo**

Listen — or your tongue will keep you deaf.

~ **Cherokee Proverb**

Friendship is held to be the severest test of character.

~ **Charles Eastman, Dakota**

Before you choose a counselor, watch him with his neighbor's children.

~ **Sioux Proverb**

I believe that every man must make his own path!

~ **Black Hawk, Sauk**

SAGE SAYINGS

The rainbow is a sign from Him who is in all things.

~ Hopi Proverb

The sky and the strong wind have moved the spirit inside me till I am carried away trembling with joy.

~ Uvavnuk Proverb

You can't purchase friendship — you have to do your part to make it.

~ Sauk Proverb

Treat less fortunate with respect as they may save your life someday.

~ Inuit Proverb

The eyes of men speak words the tongue cannot pronounce.

~ Crow Proverb

Do not look outside yourself for the leader.

~ Hopi Proverb

Do not only point the way but lead the way.

~ **Sioux Proverb**

A man must make his own arrows.

~ **Winnebago Proverb**

We are like a string of beads, all united.

~ **Hopi Proverb**

A hungry stomach makes a short prayer.

~ **Paiute Proverb**

Let me be a free man, free to travel, free to stop, free to work, free to trade where I choose, free to choose my own teachers, free to follow the religion of my fathers, free to talk, think and act for myself -- and I will obey every law or submit to the penalty.

~ **Chief Joseph, Nez Perce**

The strength of our future lies in the protecting of our past.

~ **Seminole Proverb**

Brother, you say there is but one way to worship and serve the Great Spirit. If there is but one religion, why do you white people differ so much about it? Why not all agreed, as you can all read the Book?

> ~ **Sogoyewapha, Senaca**

What happened in the past and cannot be stopped should not be lamented over.

> ~ **Pawnee Proverb**

Always be afraid of the water, ice and snow…respect them because you can not control them.

> ~ **Inuit Proverb**

Those who do not fear Great Spirit are not strong.

> ~ **Seneca Proverb**

Death always comes out of season.

> ~ **Pawnee Proverb**

When we understand deeply in our hearts, we will fear and love and know the Great Spirit.

> ~ **Lakota Proverb**

You might as well expect the rivers to run backward than to believe that any man who was born free should be contented to be penned up and denied liberty to go where he pleases.

~ Chief Joseph, Nez Perce

Love one another and do not strive for another's undoing.

~ Seneca Proverb

Know your garden.

~ Hopi Proverb

Have patience. All things change in due time. Wishing cannot bring autumn glory or cause winter to cease.

~ Ginaly-li, Cherokee

A danger foreseen is half-avoided.

~ Cheyenne Proverb

A people without faith in themselves cannot survive.

~ Hopi Proverb

Watch out for the man who says nothing and the dog who does not bark.

~ Cheyenne Proverb

The smarter a man is the more he needs God to protect him from thinking he knows everything.

~ Pima Proverb

A shark will attack you if you play alone on the beach.

~ Inuit Proverb

All who have died are equal.

~ Comanche Proverb

Sometimes I go about pitying myself and all the while I am being carried across the sky by beautiful clouds.

~ Ojibway Proverb

Brother, we do not wish to destroy your religion, or to take it from you. We only want to enjoy our own.

~ Chief Red Jacket, Seneca

Eating little and speaking little can hurt no man.

~ **Hopi Proverb**

You should water your children like you water a tree.

~ **Hopi Proverb**

Respect elders so they may add more years to your life.

~ **Inuit Proverb**

Most of us do not look as handsome to others as we do to ourselves.

~ **Assiniboine Proverb**

I have been a slave to liquor since first I tasted it—but never again will I drink any.

~ **Tenskwatawa, Shawnee**

A council fire shall be kindled for all the nations. It shall be lit for the Cherokee and the Wyandot. We will also kindle it for the seven nations living toward the sunrise, and for the nations that live toward the sunset. All shall receive the Great Law and labor together for the welfare of man.

~ **Deganawidah, Huron**

Always look at your moccasin tracks first before you speak of another's faults.

> **~ Sauk Proverb**

There is nothing as eloquent as a rattlesnakes tail.

> **~ Navajo Proverb**

Force, no matter how concealed, begets resistance.

> **~ Lakota Proverb**

Mother Earth is not a resource, she is an heirloom.

> **~ David Ipinia, Yurok**

The smarter a man is the more he needs God to protect him from thinking he knows everything.

> **~ Pima Proverb**

When you were born, you cried and the world rejoiced. Live your life so that when you die, the world cries and you rejoice.

> **~ Cherokee Proverb**

Poverty is a noose that strangles humility and breeds disrespect for God and man.

~ Sioux Proverb

Wishing cannot bring autumn glory nor cause winter to cease.

~ Kiowa Proverb

All things have inner meaning and form and power.

~ Hopi Proverb

Silence has so much meaning.

~ Yurok Proverb

All plants are our brothers and sisters. They talk to us and if we listen, we can hear them.

~ Arapaho Proverb

It is better to have less thunder in the mouth and more lightning in the hand.

~ Apache Proverb

I am one with the Earth.

> **~ Navajo Proverb**

Teaching should come from within instead of without.

> **~ Hopi Proverb**

In this world the unseen has power.

> **~ Apache Proverb**

Never sleep while your meat is cooking on the fire.

> **~ Pueblo Proverb**

The true Indian sets no price upon either his property or his labor.

> **~ Santee Proverb**

Realize that we as human beings have been put on this earth for only a short time and that we must use this time to gain wisdom, knowledge, respect and the understanding for all human beings since we are all relatives.

> **~ Cree Proverb**

A starving man will eat with the wolf.

> ~ **Unknown**

The moon is not shamed by the barking of dogs.

> ~ **Southwest Proverb**

Listen to her — our Earth, our Mother; listen to what she is saying.

> ~ **Mohawk Proverb**

Let no one say negative things about those who are not present.

> ~ **Hopi Proverb**

No tree has branches so foolish as to fight among themselves.

> ~ **Ojibway Proverb**

Only after the last tree has been cut down, Only after the last river has been poisoned, Only after the last fish has been caught, Only then will you find money cannot be eaten.

> ~ **Cree Proverb**

Our pleasures are shallow, our sorrows are deep.

> **~ Cheyenne Proverb**

The lazy man is apt to be envious.

> **~ Omaha Proverb**

We stand somewhere between the mountain and the ant.

> **~ Onondaga Proverb**

Walk lightly in the spring; Mother Earth is pregnant.

> **~ Kiowa Proverb**

Each person is his own judge.

> **~ Shawnee Proverb**

Cherish youth, but trust old age.

> **~ Pueblo Proverb**

Certain things catch your eye, but pursue only those that capture your heart.

> **~ Unknown**

Lying is a great shame.

> ~ **Sioux Proverb**

A man can't get rich if he takes proper care of his family.

> ~ **Navajo Proverb**

Dreams gather quickly like Spring crows, and they scatter.

> ~ **Simon Ortiz, Pueblo poet**

He who is present at a wrongdoing and does not lift a hand to prevent it is as guilty as the wrongdoers.

> ~ **Omaha Proverb**

Each bird loves to hear himself sing.

> ~ **Arapaho Proverb**

Truth does not happen, it just is.

> ~ **Hopi Proverb**

The mark of shame does not wash away.

> ~ **Omaha Proverb**

The earth has received the sun's hug, and we shall see the results of that love.

~ Chief Sitting Bull, Lakota

In anger a man becomes dangerous to himself and to others.

~ Omaha Proverb

Always assume your guest is tired, cold, and hungry, and act accordingly.

~ Navajo Proverb

You are never justified in arguing.

~ Hopi Proverb

In beauty it is begun. In beauty it is ended.

~ Navajo Proverb

Speak the truth in humility to all people. Only then can you be a true man.

~ Sioux Proverb

In death, I am born.

> ~ **Hopi Proverb**

One finger cannot lift a pebble.

> ~ **Hopi Proverb**

A people without a history is like the wind over buffalo grass.

> ~ **Sioux Proverb**

[Peace] comes within the souls of men when they realize their relationship, their oneness with the universe and all its powers, and when they realize that at the center of the Universe dwells the Great Spirit, and that this center is really everywhere. It is within each of us.

> ~ **Black Elk, Oglala Lakota**

Keep following a wounded animal until you get it. Leaving a wounded animal will bring bad luck. Never allow an animal to suffer.

> ~ **Inuit Proverb**

If you continue to contaminate your own home, you will eventually suffocate in your own waste.

> ~ **Lakota Proverb**

Do not allow anger to poison you.

~ Hopi Proverb

Walk on a trail of song, and all about you will be beauty.

~ Navajo Proverb

We will be known forever by the tracks we leave.

~ Dakota Proverb

Let us continue to honor that which remains only in dream memory.

~ Oneida Proverb

The Great Spirit has made us what we are.

~ Seneca Proverb

Life is both giving and receiving.

~ Mohawk Proverb

Knowledge that is not used is abused.

~ Cree Proverb

Is it wicked for me because my skin is red? Because I am Sioux? Because I would die for my people and my country?

~ **Chief Sitting Bull, Lakota**

Good words will not give me back my children.

~ **Chief Joseph, Nez Perce**

When the wisdom keepers speak, all should listen.

~ **Seneca Proverb**

I am poor and naked but I am the chief of the nation. We do not want riches but we do want to train our children right. Riches would do us no good. We could not take them with us to the other world. We do not want riches. We want peace and love.

~ **Red Cloud, Oglala Lakota**

The sea monster will put you in its amauti and take you home, if you play alone on the beach.

~ **Inuit Proverb**

A spear is a big responsibility.

~ **Navajo Proverb**

We are made from Mother Earth and we go back to Mother Earth.

~ Unknown

Give me knowledge, so I may have kindness for all.

~ Plains Proverb

To have a friend, and to be true under any and all trials, is the mark of a man.

~ Sioux Proverb

The weather will improve. It always does. Just wait patiently.

~ Inuit Proverb

True peace between nations will only happen when there is true peace within people's souls.

~ Lakota Proverb

If we wonder often, the gift of knowledge will come.

~ Arapaho Proverb

Showing kindness to a stranger is a gift that is always returned.

> ~ **Iroquois Proverb**

Those who have one foot in the canoe, and one foot in the boat, are going to fall into the river.

> ~ **Tuscarora Proverb**

Coyote is always out there waiting, and Coyote is always hungry.

> ~ **Navajo Proverb**

Let your nature be known and expressed.

> ~ **Huron Proverb**

Talk to your children while they are eating; what you say will stay even after you are gone.

> ~ **Nez Perce Proverb**

Rituals must be performed with good and pure hearts.

> ~ **Hopi Proverb**

SAGE SAYINGS

There is no fear when there is faith.

~ **Kiowa Proverb**

Humankind has not woven the web of life. We are but one thread within it. Whatever we do to the web, we do to ourselves. All things are bound together. All things connect.

~ **Chief Seattle, Duwamish**

I grew up knowing it's wrong to have more than you need. It means you're not taking care of your people.

~ **Navajo Proverb**

The one who tells the stories rules the world.

~ **Hopi Proverb**

In the old days we used to respect everything… This isn't done today, that's why we are lost.

~ **Isiah Bear, Muskoday First Nation**

When asked to do something, we were to do it no matter how lazy we felt. It's important not to ignore what we are told to do.

~ **Inuit Proverb**

I have seen that in any great undertaking it is not enough for a man to depend simply upon himself.

~ **Isna-la-wica, Teton Sioux**

If you borrow a rifle, at least clean it after use.

~ **Inuit Proverb**

Don't make fun of people that may be different.

~ **Inuit Proverb**

You must speak straight so that your words may go as sunlight into our hearts.

~ **Cochise, Chiricahua Apache**

We also have a religion that was given to our forefathers, and has been handed down to us, their children. It teaches us to be thankful, to be united, and to love one another. We never quarrel about religion.

~ **Red Jacket**

Listen to the voice of nature, for it holds treasures for you.

~ **Huron Proverb**

We have a responsibility to give something back.

~ **Cherokee Proverb**

There is no warning for upcoming danger.

~ **Cheyenne Proverb**

What is life? It is the flash of a firefly in the night. It is the breath of a buffalo in the wintertime. It is the little shadow which runs across the grass and loses itself in the sunset.

~ **Crowfoot, Blackfoot**

Day and night cannot dwell together.

~ **Duwamish Proverb**

Now, look into the Light and breathe deeply the joy of life.

~ **Hopi Proverb**

Thoughts are like arrows; once released, they strike their mark. Guard them well or one day you may be your own victim.

~ **Navajo Proverb**

No river can return to its source, yet all rivers must have a beginning.

~ Unknown

If we wonder often, the gift of knowledge will come.

~ Arapaho Proverb

Like a seed, your future is only beginning to emerge out of the darkness.

~ Hopi Proverb

The pipe is here to unite us, to remove the fences people put up against one another.

~ Leonard Crow Dog, Lakota

What good will it do you to take by force that which you may have by love?

~ Powhatan (father of Pocahontas)

An angry word is like striking with a knife.

~ Hopi Proverb

Let your nature be known and proclaimed.

~ Huron Proverb

The clear sky and the green fruitful Earth are good; but peace among men is better.

~ Omaha Proverb

Grown men can learn from very little children for the hearts of the little children are pure.

~ Black Elk, Oglala Lakota

We should only think of beautiful things when we look at other people.

~ Rolling Thunder, Cherokee

Man's heart away from nature becomes hard.

~ Standing Bear

Ask questions from you heart and you will be answered from the heart.

~ Omaha Proverb

When a favor is shown to a white man, he feels it in his head and the tongue speaks out; when a kindness is shown to an Indian, he feels it in his heart and the heart has no tongue.

~ **Shosphone Proverb**

We are the ones we've been waiting for.

~ **Hopi Proverb**

It takes a thousand voices to tell a single story.

~ **Nez Perce Proverb**

We know our lands have now become more valuable. The white people think we do not know their value; but we know that the land is everlasting, and the few goods we receive for it are soon worn out and gone.

~ **Canassatego, Onondaga**

Native American isn't blood. It is what is in the heart. The love for the land, the respect for it, those who inhabit it, and the respect and acknowledgement of the spirits and elders. That is what it is to be Indian.

~ **White Feather, Navajo Medicine Man**

In my tradition, to be noble is to give to those who have less. It is an issue of service and leadership.

~ Norbert Hill, Oneida

It is less of a problem to be poor, than to be dishonest.

~ Anishinabe Proverb

Even as you desire good treatment, so render it.

~ Seneca Proverb

It is good to be reminded that each of us has a different dream.

~ Crow Proverb

Everyone who is successful must have dreamed of something.

~ Maricopa Proverb

It is no longer good enough to cry peace, we must act peace, live peace and live in peace.

~ Unknown

Create your community.

> ~ **Hopi Proverb**

It is easy to show braveness from a safe distance.

> ~ **Omaha Proverb**

What the people believe is true.

> ~ **Anishinabe Proverb**

A brave man dies but once, a coward many times.

> ~ **Iowa Proverb**

Our land is everything to us... I will tell you one of the things we remember on our land. We remember that our grandfathers paid for it - with their lives.

> ~ **John Wooden Legs, Cheyenne**

Don't walk behind me; I may not lead. Don't walk in front of me; I may not follow. Walk beside me that we may be as one.

> ~ **Ute Proverb**

All that we do must be done in a sacred manner and in celebration.

~ Hopi Proverb

May our thoughts reach the sky where there is holiness.

~ Arapaho Proverb

When you have a talent of any kind, use it, take care of it, guard it.

~ Sauk Proverb

Always make room for elders. i.e. Give your chair to an older person.

~ Inuit Proverb

I was eager to learn and to do things, and thus I learned quickly.

~ Chief Sitting Bull, Lakota

No man can think for me.

~ Chief Joseph, Nez Perce

If your eye lids keep moving by themselves (twitching), you will very shortly, meet the person who is thinking of you.

~ Inuit Proverb

If a man is to do something more than human, he must have more than human powers.

~ Unknown

The clear sky and the green fruitful Earth are good; but peace among men is better.

~ Omaha Proverb

All birds, even those of the same species, are not alike, and it is the same with animals and with human beings. The reason WakanTanka does not make two birds, or animals, or human beings exactly alike is because each is placed here by WakanTanka to be an independent individuality and to rely upon itself.

~ Shooter, Lakota

Wisdom comes only when you stop looking for it and start living the life the Creator intended for you.

~ Hopi Proverb

SAGE SAYINGS

Visit your elders. You will live longer.

~ Inuit Proverb

One has to face fear or forever run from it.

~ Crow Proverb

From a grain of sand to a great mountain, all is sacred.

~ Peter Blue Cloud, Mohawk

Civilization has been thrust upon me, and it has not added one whit to my love for truth, honesty, and generosity.

~ Chief Luther Standing Bear, Oglala Lakota

When it comes time to die, be not like those whose hearts are filled with the fear of death, so when their time comes they weep and pray for a little more time to live their lives over again in a different way. Sing your death song, and die like a hero going home.

~ Chief Aupumut, Mohican

He who would do great things should not attempt them all alone.

~ Seneca Proverb

are not dead who live in the hearts they leave behind.

~ **Tuscarora Proverb**

Peace and happiness are available in every moment. Peace is every step. We shall walk hand in hand. There are no political solutions to spiritual problems. Remember: If the Creator put it there, it is in the right place. The soul would have no rainbow if the eyes had no tears.

~ **Unknown**

Listen with your heart. Learn from your experiences, and always be open to new ones.

~ **Cherokee Proverb**

Misfortune happens even to the wisest and best men.

~ **Omaha Proverb**

The more often you ask how much farther you have to go, the longer your quest will feel.

~ **Senaca Proverb**

Music is a healing force – all living spirits sing.

~ **Joanna Shenandoah, Oneida composer**

I will never let my culture go! I fear for our young people. I hope they have enough sense to seek spiritual guidance from the elders

~ Edward Fox, Sweetgrass First Nation

May the Great Spirit always give you blessings.

~ Geronimo, Chiracahua Apache

An overly loved person will encounter polar bears more than those who are not.

~ Inuit Proverb

If a man is as wise as a serpent, he can afford to be as harmless as a dove.

~ Cheyenne Proverb

O' Great Spirit, I want no blood upon my land to stain the grass. I want it all clear and pure, and I wish it so, that all who go through among my people may find it peaceful when they come, and leave peacefully when they go.

~ Ten Bears, Yamparika Comanche

Time discovered truth.

~ Seneca Proverb

If your lips keep twitching by themselves, then someone is talking about you.

> ~ **Inuit Proverb**

Sometimes dreams are wiser than waking.

> ~ **Oglala Lakota Proverb**

A man or woman with many children has many homes.

> ~ **Lakota Proverb**

Each man is good in His sight. It is not necessary for eagles to be crows.

> ~ **Chief Sitting Bull, Lakota**

Like the grasses showing tender faces to each other, thus should we do, for this was the wish of the Grandfathers of the World.

> ~ **Black Elk, Oglala Lakota**

Don't be afraid to cry. It will free your mind of sorrowful thoughts.

> ~ **Hopi Proverb**

Some people are smart but not wise.

> **~ Shosphone Proverb**

If you wonder often, the gift of understanding will come.

> **~ Arapaho Proverb**

Trouble no one about their religion.

> **~ Chief Tecumseh, Shawnee**

Misfortune will happen to the wisest and best of men.

> **~ Pawnee Proverb**

Don't let yesterday use up too much of today.

> **~ Cherokee Proverb**

Love yourself; get outside yourself and take action. Focus on the solution; be at peace.

> **~ Sioux Proverb**

SHARE YOUR SAYINGS

This compilation includes about 500 sayings we discovered. We know there are many more worthy of reading and we welcome suggested additions. Please share your favorite sayings with us. We are working on a series of follow-on projects and we would be delighted to include sayings from our readers. Send the sayings to sayings@sagesayings.info

OFFER YOUR CORRECTIONS

Please help us make the collection more accurate by contacting us with any information that you have about our errors, omissions, or misrepresentations.

CONNECT WITH JOHN & JOANN

We hope that you will want to connect with us. The easiest way is to visit our companion website, Sage Saying (www.sagesayings.info). Please feel free to visit John's professional speaking site: www.johngirard.net. We welcome your feedback about any of our sites or the book. Our email addresses are john@sagesayings.info and joann@sagesayings.info

ABOUT THE PEOPLE

As we mentioned in the introduction, as interesting as we find *the sage sayings*, perhaps the most fascinating exploration is the people behind the words. As we read their works we cannot help but notice their common sense, connection to the planet, and recognition of family. These important ideas seem to be lost in many of the decisions that are made in the 24/7 ever connected world in which so many of us live and work. We wonder if the next generations of readers will think we were so wise.

The brief overviews that follow are all from Wikipedia and used in accordance with their Terms of Use and the Creative Commons Deed. We provide them as quick reference but hope that they serve as a catalyst for more research. We appreciate Wikipedia making this information available and encourage you to visit *The People's Encyclopedia* to continue your voyage of discovery. In some cases the entries have been tweaked ever so slightly; however, in all cases a link for the original entry is included.

Please remember this book is licensed under the Creative Commons Attribution 4.0 International License. Please see http://creativecommons.org/licenses/by/4.0/ to learn more about how you may share and adapt the book.

Abenaki

The Abenaki (Abnaki, Wabanaki, Waponahki) are a tribe of Native American and First Nations people, one of the Algonquian-speaking peoples of northeastern North America. The Abenaki live in the New England region of the United States and Quebec and the Maritimes of Canada, a region called *Wabanaki* ("Dawn Land") in the Eastern Algonquian languages. The Abenaki are one of the five members of the Wabanaki Confederacy. "Abenaki" is a linguistic and geographic grouping; historically there was not a strong central authority, but as listed below a large number of smaller bands and tribes who shared many cultural traits.

http://en.wikipedia.org/wiki/Abenaki

Anishinaabe

The meaning of *Anishnaabeg* is 'First' or 'Original Peoples'. Another definition - possibly reflecting a traditionalist's viewpoint with a certain moral dimension - refers to "the good humans", or good people, meaning those who are on the right road/path given to them by the Creator or *Gichi-Manidoo* (Great Spirit). The Ojibwe people who moved to what are now the prairie provinces of Canada call themselves *Nakawē(-k)* and their branch of the Anishinaabe language, *Nakawēmowin*. (The French ethnonym for the group was the *Saulteaux*). Particular Anishinaabeg groups have different names from region to region.

http://en.wikipedia.org/wiki/Anishinabe

Apache

Apache is the collective term for several culturally related groups of Native Americans in the United States originally from the Southwest United States. These indigenous peoples of North America speak a Southern Athabaskan (Apachean) language, which is related linguistically to the languages of Athabaskan speakers of Alaska and western Canada.

http://en.wikipedia.org/wiki/Apache

Arapaho

The Arapaho (in French: *Arapahos, Gens de Vache*) are a tribe of Native Americans historically living on the plains of Colorado and Wyoming. They were close allies of the Cheyenne tribe and loosely aligned with the Lakota and Dakota. The Arapaho language, *Heenetiit*, is an Algonquian language closely related to Gros Ventre (Ahe/A'ananin), whose people are seen as an early offshoot of the Arapaho. Blackfeet and Cheyenne are the other Algonquian-speakers on the Plains, but their languages are quite different from Arapaho.

http://en.wikipedia.org/wiki/Arapaho

Arikara

Arikara (also Sahnish, The Arikara call themselves Sahnish, Arikaree, Ree) are a group of Native Americans in North Dakota. Today they are enrolled in the federally recognized tribe the Three Affiliated Tribes of the Fort Berthold Reservation. (see Three Affiliated Tribes entry below)

http://en.wikipedia.org/wiki/Arikara_people

Assiniboine

The Assiniboine or Assiniboin people, also known as the Hohe and known by the endonym Nakota (or Nakoda or

Nakona), are a Siouan First Nations/Native American people originally from the Northern Great Plains of North America. Today, they are centered in present-day Saskatchewan, but they have also populated parts of Alberta, southwestern Manitoba, northern Montana and western North Dakota. They were well known throughout much of the late 18th and early 19th century.

http://en.wikipedia.org/wiki/Assiniboine_people

Blackfoot

The Blackfoot Confederacy or Niitsítapi (meaning "original people") is the collective name of three First Nations bands in Alberta, Canada and one Native American tribe in Montana, United States. Historically, the member peoples of the Confederacy were nomadic bison hunters, who ranged across large areas of the northern Great Plains of Western North America, specifically the semi-arid short-grass prairie ecological region. In the first half of the 18th century, they adopted horses and firearms acquired from European-descended traders and their Cree and Assiniboine resellers. With these new tools, the Blackfoot expanded their territory at the expense of neighboring peoples. Through the use of horses, Blackfoot and other Plains peoples harvested bison at a much-accelerated rate.

http://en.wikipedia.org/wiki/Blackfoot_Confederacy

Cherokee

The Cherokee are a Native American people historically settled in the Southeastern United States (principally Georgia, North Carolina, South Carolina, and East Tennessee). They speak an Iroquoian language. In the 19th century, historians and ethnographers recorded their oral tradition that told of the tribe having migrated south in ancient times from the Great Lakes region, where other Iroquoian-speaking peoples were. They began to have contact with European traders in the 18th century.

http://en.wikipedia.org/wiki/Cherokee

Cheyenne

The Cheyenne people are an indigenous people of the Great Plains, and are considered to be part of the Algonquian language–speaking people. The Cheyenne are made up of two Native American ethnic groups, the Só'taeo'o (more commonly spelled as Suhtai or Sutaio) and the Tsétsêhéstâhese (also spelled Tsitsistas). These tribes merged in the early 19th century. Today the Cheyenne people are split into two federally recognized groups: Southern Cheyenne, who are enrolled in the Cheyenne and Arapaho Tribes in Oklahoma, and the Northern Cheyenne, who are enrolled in the Northern Cheyenne Tribe of the Northern Cheyenne Indian Reservation in Montana.

http://en.wikipedia.org/wiki/Cheyenne_people

Chippewa - see Ojibwe

Chiricahua

Chiricahua is a group of Apache Native Americans who live in the Southwest United States. At the time of European encounter, they were living in 15 million acres (61,000 km^2) of territory in southwestern New Mexico and southeastern Arizona in the United States, and in northern Sonora and Chihuahua in Mexico. Today, only two tribes of the Chiricahua Apache located in the United States are federally recognized: the Fort Sill Apache Tribe, located near Apache, Oklahoma; and the Chiricahua tribe located on the Mescalero Apache reservation near Ruidoso, New

Mexico.

http://en.wikipedia.org/wiki/Chiricahua

Comanche

The Comanche (Comanche: *Numunuu*) are a Plains Indian tribe whose historic territory, known as Comancheria, consisted of present day eastern New Mexico, southeastern Colorado, southwestern Kansas, western Oklahoma, and most of northwest Texas. The Comanche people are federally recognized as the Comanche Nation, headquartered in Lawton, Oklahoma. Post-contact, the Comanches were hunter-gatherers with a horse culture. There may have been as many as 45,000 Comanches in the late 18th century. They were the dominant tribe on the Southern Plains and often took captives from weaker tribes during warfare, selling them as slaves to the Spanish and later Mexican settlers. They also took thousands of captives from the Spanish, Mexican and American settlers.

http://en.wikipedia.org/wiki/Comanche

Conestoga - see **Susquehannock**

Crow

The Crow, called the Apsáalooke in their own Siouan language, or variants including Absaroka, are Native Americans, who in historical times lived in the Yellowstone River valley, which extends from present-day Wyoming, through Montana and into North Dakota, where it joins the Missouri River. Today, they are enrolled in the federally recognized Crow Tribe of Montana. The Crow were generally friendly with the whites and managed to retain a large reservation of over 9300 sq km despite territorial losses.

http://en.wikipedia.org/wiki/Crow_Nation

Dakota

The Dakota people are an indigenous people of the Great Plains of Canada and the United States. They are one of the three main subcultures of the Sioux people, and are usually divided into the Eastern Dakota and the Western Dakota. The Eastern Dakota are the Santee (*Isáŋyathi* or *Isáŋathi*; "Knife"), who reside in the extreme east of the Dakotas, Minnesota and northern Iowa. The Western Dakota are the Yankton and the Yanktonai (*Iháŋktȟuŋwaŋ* and *Iháŋktȟuŋwaŋna*; "Village-at-the-end" and "Little village-at-the-end"), who reside in the Minnesota River area. The Yankton-Yanktonai are collectively also referred to by the endonym *Wičhíyena*, and have in the past been erroneously classified as Nakota.

http://en.wikipedia.org/wiki/Dakota_people

Delaware - see Lenape

Duwamish

The Duwamish are a Lushootseed Native American tribe in western Washington, and the indigenous people of metropolitan Seattle, where they have been living since the end of the last glacial period (c. 8000 BCE, 10,000 years ago). The Duwamish tribe descends from at least two distinct groups from before intense contact with people of European ancestry—the *People of the Inside* (the environs of Elliott Bay) and the *People of the Large Lake* (Lake Washington)—and continues to evolve both culturally and ethnically. By historic language, the Duwamish are (Skagit-Nisqually) Lushootseed; Lushootseed is a Salishan language.

http://en.wikipedia.org/wiki/Duwamish_tribe

Ho-Chunk

The Ho-Chunk, also known as Winnebago, are a Siouan-speaking tribe of Native Americans, native to the present-day states of Wisconsin, Minnesota, and parts of Iowa and Illinois. Today the two federally recognized Ho-Chunk tribes, the Ho-Chunk Nation of Wisconsin and Winnebago Tribe of Nebraska, have territory primarily within the states included in their names.

http://en.wikipedia.org/wiki/Ho-Chunk

Hopi

The Hopi are a federally recognized tribe of Native American people, who primarily live on the 2,531.773 sq mi (6,557.26 km²) Hopi Reservation in northeastern Arizona. As of 2010, there were 18,327 Hopi in the United States, according to the 2010 census. The Hopi language is one of the 30 of the Uto-Aztecan language family. The Hopi Reservation is entirely surrounded by the much larger Navajo Reservation. The two nations used to share the *Navajo-Hopi Joint Use Area*, but this was a source of conflict. The partition of this area, commonly known as Big Mountain, by Acts of Congress in 1974 and 1996, has also resulted in long-term controversy.

http://en.wikipedia.org/wiki/Hopi_people

Huron - see Wyandot

Inuit

Inuit (Inuktitut: ᐃᓄᐃᑦ, "the people") are a group of culturally similar indigenous peoples inhabiting the Arctic regions of Greenland, Canada, and the United States. Inuit is a plural noun; the singular is Inuk. The Inuit languages are classified in the Eskimo-Aleut family. In the United States, the term "Eskimo" was commonly used to describe Inuit, and other Arctic peoples, because it includes both of Alaska's Yupik and Iñupiat peoples while "Inuit" is not proper or accepted as a term for the Yupik. No collective term exists for both peoples other than "Eskimo." However, Aboriginal peoples in Canada and Greenland view the name as pejorative, so "Inuit" has become more common.

http://en.wikipedia.org/wiki/Inuit

Iowa

The Iowa (also spelled Ioway), also known as the Báxoje, are a Native American Siouan people. Today they are enrolled in either of two federally recognized tribes, the Iowa Tribe of Oklahoma and the Iowa Tribe of Kansas and Nebraska. With the Missouria and the Otoe, the Ioway are the Chiwere-speaking peoples, claiming the Ho-Chunks as their "grandfathers." Their estimated population of 1,100 (in 1760) dropped to 800 (in 1804), a decrease caused mainly by smallpox, to which they had no natural immunity. In 1824, the Iowa were moved from Iowa to reservations in Brown County, Kansas, and Richardson County, Nebraska. Bands of Iowa moved to Indian Territory in the late 19th century and settled south of Perkins, Oklahoma, becoming the Iowa Tribe of Oklahoma.

http://en.wikipedia.org/wiki/Iowa_people

Iroquois

The Iroquois, also known as the Haudenosaunee, or the Six Nations, (the Five Nations and *Five Nations of the Iroquois* before 1722), and to themselves the

Goano'ganoch'sa'jeh'seroni or Ganonsyoni. A historically powerful and important northeast Native American people who formed the Iroquois Confederacy and today make up the Six Nations. Many prominent individuals are Iroquois or have Iroquois ancestry. A melting pot culture, vibrant today in language, culture, and independent governance. In 2010, more than 45,000 enrolled Six Nations people lived in Canada, and about 80,000 in the United States.

http://en.wikipedia.org/wiki/Iroquois

Kiowa

The Kiowa are a nation of American Indians of the Great Plains. They migrated from western Montana southward into the Rocky Mountains in Colorado in the 17th and 18th centuries, and finally into the Southern Plains by the early 19th century. In 1867, the Kiowa moved to a reservation in southwestern Oklahoma. Today they are federally recognized as Kiowa Tribe of Oklahoma with headquarters in Carnegie, Oklahoma. The Kiowa language is still spoken today and is part of the Tanoan language family. As of 2011, there are 12,000 members.

http://en.wikipedia.org/wiki/Kiowa_people

Lakota

The Lakota people (also known as Teton, Titunwan ("prairie dwellers"), Teton Sioux ("snake, or enemy") are an indigenous people of the Great Plains of North America. They are part of a confederation of seven related Sioux tribes, the Očhéthi Šakówiŋ or seven council fires, and speak Lakota, one of the three major dialects of the Sioux language. The Lakota are the westernmost of the three Siouan language groups, occupying lands in both North and South Dakota.

http://en.wikipedia.org/wiki/Lakota_people

Lenape

The Lenape are Native American peoples now living in Canada and the United States. They are also called Delaware Indians after their historic territory along the frequently mountainous landscapes flanking the Delaware River watershed. As a result of disruptions and political will of the white population following the American Revolutionary War and later developments such as the oft-voiced attitudes later termed manifest destiny, which in part led to the Indian removals from the eastern United States, the main groups now live in Ontario (Canada), Wisconsin, and Oklahoma.

http://en.wikipedia.org/wiki/Lenape

Lumbee

The Lumbee Tribe of North Carolina is a state recognized tribe of approximately 55,000 enrolled members, most of them living in Robeson and the adjacent counties in southeastern North Carolina. The Lumbee Tribe is the largest tribe in North Carolina, the largest tribe east of the Mississippi River and the ninth largest non-federally recognized group in the nation. According to the 2000 US Census report, Pembroke, North Carolina, is made up of 89% Lumbee Indian and the population of Robeson County is almost 40% Lumbee.

http://en.wikipedia.org/wiki/Lumbee

Maricopa

The Maricopa or Piipaash, are a Native American tribe, who live in the Salt River Pima-Maricopa Indian Community and Gila River Indian Community along with the Pima, a tribe with whom the Maricopa have long held a positive relationship. The Maricopa, mostly Xalychidom Piipaash, at the Salt River Pima-Maricopa Indian Community are concentrated in Lehi, while the Maricopa at the Gila River Indian Communityare concentrated in Maricopa Colony. The Maricopa are a River Yuman group, formerly living along the banks of the Colorado River.

http://en.wikipedia.org/wiki/Maricopa_people

Miniconjou

The Miniconjou (Lakota: Mnikȟówožu, Hokwoju - 'Plants by the Water') are a Native American people constituting a subdivision of the Lakota people, who formerly inhabited an area in western present-day South Dakota from the Black Hills in to the Platte River. The contemporary population lives mostly in west-central South Dakota. Perhaps the most famous Miniconjou chief was Touch the Clouds.

http://en.wikipedia.org/wiki/Minniconjou

Minquass - see Susquehannock

Mohawk

The Kanien'kehá:ka or Mohawk people are the most easterly tribe of the Iroquois Confederacy. They are the People of "Ka Nee-en Ka" (or "Flint Stone Place") and are an Iroquoian-speaking indigenous people of North America. They were historically based in the Mohawk Valley in upstate New York; their territory ranged to present-day southern Quebec and eastern Ontario. Their traditional homeland stretched southward of the Mohawk River, eastward to the Green Mountains of Vermont, westward to the border with the Oneida Nation's traditional homeland territory, and northward to the St

Lawrence River. Their current settlements include areas around Lake Ontario and the St Lawrence River in Canada and New York.

http://en.wikipedia.org/wiki/Mohawk_people

Mohican

The Mahican (also Mohican) are an Eastern Algonquian Native American tribe, originally settled in the Hudson River Valley (around Albany, NY) and western New England. After 1680, many moved to Stockbridge, Massachusetts. Since the 1830s, most descendants of the Mahican are located in Shawano County, Wisconsin, where they formed the federally recognized Stockbridge-Munsee Community with Lenape people and have a 22,000-acre (8,900 ha) reservation.

http://en.wikipedia.org/wiki/Mohican

Muskoday

The Muskoday First Nation (formerly the John Smith First Nation) is a First Nation in Saskatchewan, Canada, composed of Cree and Saulteaux peoples. The First Nation has a registered population of 1552 people as of December 2007, of which approximately 560 members of the First Nation live on-reserve, and approximately 980 live off-reserve. Muskoday's territory is located in the aspen parkland biome. It is bordered by the rural municipalities of Birch Hills No. 460 and Prince Albert No. 461.

http://en.wikipedia.org/wiki/Muskoday_First_Nation

Navajo

The Navajo (Navajo: *Diné* or *Naabeehó*) of the

Southwestern United States are the largest federally recognized tribe of the United States of America with 300,048 enrolled tribal members. The Navajo Nation constitutes an independent governmental body, which manages the Navajo Indian reservation in the Four Corners area of the United States. The Navajo language is spoken throughout the region with most Navajo capable of speaking English as well. As of 2011, the states with the largest Navajo populations are Arizona (140,263), and New Mexico (108,306). Over three-quarters of the Navajo population reside in these two states.

http://en.wikipedia.org/wiki/Navajo_people

Nootka

The Nuu-chah-nulth, also formerly referred to as the Nootka, Nutka, Aht, Nuuchahnulth, are one of the Indigenous peoples of the Pacific Northwest Coast of Canada. The term 'Nuu-chah-nulth' is used to describe fifteen separate but related nations, such as the Nuchatlaht First Nation, whose traditional home is in the Pacific Northwest on the west coast of Vancouver Island. In precontact and early post-contact times, the number of nations was much greater, but smallpox and other consequences of contact resulted in the disappearance of some groups and the absorption of others into neighboring groups.

http://en.wikipedia.org/wiki/Nuu-chah-nulth_people

Nuxalk

The Nuxalk people (Nuxalk: *Nuxálk*), also referred to as the Bella Coola or Bellacoola, are an Indigenous First Nation in Canada, living in the area in and around Bella Coola, British Columbia. Their language is also called Nuxalk. Their tribal government is the Nuxalk Nation.

SAGE SAYINGS

The name "Bella Coola", often used in academic writing, is not preferred by the Nuxálk; it is thought to be a derivation of the neighboring coastal Heiltsuk people's name for the Nuxálk, *bḷ́xʷlá* (rendered *plxwlaq's* in Nuxalk orthography), meaning "stranger".

http://en.wikipedia.org/wiki/Nuxalk_people

Oglala Lakota

The Oglala Lakota or Oglala Sioux (pronounced [oɡə'lala], meaning "to scatter one's own" in Lakota language) are one of the seven subtribes of the Lakota people, who along with the Nakota and Dakota, make up the Great Sioux Nation. A majority of the Oglala live on the Pine Ridge Indian Reservation in South Dakota, the eighth-largest Native American reservation in the United States. The Oglala are a federally recognized tribe whose official title is the Oglala Sioux Tribe (previously called the Oglala Sioux Tribe of the Pine Ridge Reservation, South Dakota).

http://en.wikipedia.org/wiki/Oglala_Lakota

Ojibwe

The Ojibwe (also *Ojibwa*), Anishinaabe, or Chippewa are one of the largest groups of Native American and First Nations Peoples on the North American continent. There are Ojibwe communities in both Canada and the United States. In Canada, they are the second-largest population among First Nations, surpassed only by the Cree. In the United States, they have the fourth-largest population among Native American tribes, surpassed only by the Navajo, Cherokee and Lakota

http://en.wikipedia.org/wiki/Chippewa

Omaha

The Omaha are a federally recognized Native American tribe that lives on the Omaha Reservation in northeastern Nebraska and western Iowa, United States. They Omaha people migrated to the upper Missouri area and the Plains by the late 17th century from earlier locations in the Ohio River Valley. The Omaha speak a Siouan language of the Dhegihan branch, which is very similar to that spoken by the Ponca. The latter were part of the Omaha before splitting off into a separate tribe in the mid-18th century. They were also related to the Siouan-speaking Osage, Quapaw, and Kansapeoples, who also migrated west under pressure from the Iroquois in the Ohio Valley. After pushing out other tribes, the Iroquois kept control of the area as a hunting ground.

http://en.wikipedia.org/wiki/Omaha_people

Oneida

The Oneida (*Onҫ yóte'* or *Onayotekaono*, meaning "Upright Stone Place, or standing stone", *Thwahrù nҫ'* in Tuscarora) are a Native American/First Nations people; they are one of the five founding nations of the Iroquois Confederacy in the area of upstate New York. The Iroquois call themselves *Haudenosaunee* ("The people of the longhouses") in reference to their communal lifestyle and the construction of their dwellings. After the American Revolutionary War, they were forced to cede all but 300,000 acres (1,200 km^2), and were later forced to cede more. Under federal and state pressure, many Oneida resettled in Wisconsin in the early 1800s. Others who had allied with the British had already migrated to Canada.

http://en.wikipedia.org/wiki/Oneida_people

Onondaga

The Onondaga (*Onöñda'gega'* or "Hill Place") People are one of the original five constituent nations of the Iroquois (*Haudenosaunee*) Confederacy. Their traditional homeland is in and around Onondaga County, New York. Known as *Gana'dagwëni:io'geh* to the other Iroquois tribes, this name allows people to know the difference when talking about Onondaga in Six Nations, Ontario or near Syracuse, New York. Being centrally located, they were considered the "Keepers of the Fire" (*Kayečisnakwe'nì yu'* in Tuscarora) in the figurative longhouse. The Cayuga and Seneca had territory to their west and the Oneida and Mohawk to their east. For this reason, the League of the Iroquois historically met at the Iroquois government's capital at Onondaga, as indeed the traditional chiefs do today.

http://en.wikipedia.org/wiki/Onondaga_people

Osage

The Osage Nation is a Native American Siouan-speaking tribe in the United States that originated in the Ohio River valley in present-day Kentucky. After years of war with the invading Iroquois, the Osage migrated west of the Mississippi River to their historic lands in present-day Arkansas, Missouri, Kansas, and Oklahoma by the mid-17th century. At the height of their power in the early 18th century, the Osage had become the dominant power in their region, controlling the area between the Missouri and Red rivers. They are a federally recognized tribe and based mainly in Osage County, Oklahoma, coterminous with their reservation. Members are found throughout the country.

http://en.wikipedia.org/wiki/Osage_Nation

Paiute

Paiute (also Piute) refers to three closely related groups of indigenous peoples of the Great Basin: Northern Paiute of California, Idaho, Nevada and Oregon; Owens Valley Paiute of California and Nevada; and Southern Paiute of Arizona, southeastern California and Nevada, and Utah. The origin of the word *Paiute* is unclear. Some anthropologists have interpreted it as "Water Ute" or "True Ute". The Northern Paiute call themselves *Numa* (sometimes written *Numu*); the Southern Paiute call themselves *Nuwuvi*; both terms mean "the people". The Northern Paiute are sometimes referred to as *Paviotso*. Early Euro-American settlers often referred to both groups of Paiute as "Diggers" (presumably because of their practice of digging for roots for food). As the Paiute consider the term derogatory, they discourage its use.

http://en.wikipedia.org/wiki/Paiute_people

Pawnee

Pawnee people (also Paneassa, Pari, Pariki) are a Caddoan-speaking Native American tribe. They are federally recognized as the Pawnee Nation of Oklahoma and have four confederated bands: the Chaui, Kitkehakhi, Pitahawirata, and Skidi. Historically, the Pawnee lived along outlying tributaries of the Missouri River: the Platte, Loup and Republican rivers in present-day Nebraska and in northern Kansas. They lived in permanent earth lodge villages where they farmed. They left the villages on seasonal buffalo hunts, using tipis while traveling.

http://en.wikipedia.org/wiki/Pawnee_people

Pima

The Pima (or Akimel O'odham also spelled Akimel

O'otham - "the kaka , formerly oft simply known as *Pima*) are a group of Indigenous Americans living in an area consisting of what is now central and southern Arizona. Currently the majority population of the surviving two bands of the Akimel O'odham is based in two reservations - the *Keli Akimel O'otham* on the Gila River Indian Community (GRIC) and the *On'k Akimel O'odham* on the Salt River Pima-Maricopa Indian Community (SRPMIC).

http://en.wikipedia.org/wiki/Pima_people

Plains

The Plains Indians are the indigenous peoples who live on the plains and rolling hills of the Great Plains of North America. Their equestrian culture and resistance to domination by Canada and the United States have made the Plains Indians an archetype in literature and art for American Indians everywhere. Plains Indians are usually divided into two broad classifications which overlap to some degree. The first group became fully nomadic and dependent upon the horse during the 18th and 19th centuries, following the vast herds of buffalo, although some tribes occasionally engaged in agriculture; growing tobacco and corn primarily. These include the Blackfoot, Arapaho, Assiniboine, Cheyenne, Comanche, Crow, Gros Ventre, Kiowa, Lakota, Lipan, Plains Apache (or Kiowa Apache), Plains Cree, Plains Ojibwe, Sarsi, Nakoda (Stoney), and Tonkawa.

http://en.wikipedia.org/wiki/Plains_Indians

Ponca

The Ponca (Pá^{n}ka iyé: Pá^{n}ka or Ppá^{n}kka pronounced) are a Native American people of the Dhegihan branch of the Siouan-language group. There are two federally recognized Ponca tribes: the Ponca Tribe of Nebraska and the Ponca

Tribe of Indians of Oklahoma. Their traditions and historical accounts suggest they originated as a tribe east of the Mississippi River in the Ohio River valley area and migrated west for game and as a result of Iroquois wars.

http://en.wikipedia.org/wiki/Ponca

Potawatomi

The Potawatomi, also spelled Pottawatomie and Pottawatomi (among many variations), are a Native American people of the upper Mississippi River region. They traditionally speak the Potawatomi language, a member of the Algonquian family. In the Potawatomi language, they generally call themselves *Bodéwadmi*, a name that means "keepers of the fire" and that was applied to them by their Ojibwe brothers. They originally called themselves *Neshnabé*, a cognate of the word *Anishinaabe*. The Potawatomi were part of a long-term alliance, called the Council of Three Fires, with the Ojibwe/Jibwe (Chippewa) and Odaawaa/[O]dawa (Ottawa). In the Council of Three Fires, the Potawatomi were considered the "youngest brother."

http://en.wikipedia.org/wiki/Potawatomi

Pueblo

The Pueblo people are Native American people in the Southwestern United States comprising several different language groups and two major cultural divisions, one organized by matrilineal kinship systems and the other having a patrilineal system. These determine the clan membership of children, and lines of inheritance and descent. Their traditional economy is based on agriculture and trade. At the time of Spanish encounter in the 16th century, they were living in villages that the Spanish called *pueblos*, meaning "towns". Of the 21 surviving pueblos in the 21st century, Taos, Acoma, Zuni, and Hopi are the best-known. The main pueblos are located primarily in the present-day states of New Mexico and Arizona.

http://en.wikipedia.org/wiki/Puebloan_peoples

Santee - see **Dakota**

Sauk

The Sacs or Sauks are a group of Native Americans of the Eastern Woodlands culture group. The Sauk are believed to have had their original territory along the St. Lawrence River. They were driven by pressure from other tribes, especially the Iroquois, to migrate to Michigan, where they settled around Saginaw Bay. Due to the yellow-clay soils found around Saginaw Bay, their autonym was *Oθaakiiwaki* (often interpreted to mean "yellow-earth".) The Ojibwe and Ottawa name for the tribe (exonym) was *Ozaagii*, meaning "those at the outlet". From the sound of that, the French derived *Sac* and the English "Sauk".

http://en.wikipedia.org/wiki/Sauk_people

Seminole

The Seminoles are a Native American people originally of Florida. Today, most Seminoles live in Oklahoma with a minority in Florida; there are three federally recognized tribes and independent groups. The Seminole nation emerged in a process of ethnogenesis out of groups of Native Americans, most significantly Creek from what are now northern Florida, Georgia, and Alabama, who settled in Florida in the early 18th century. The word *Seminole* is a corruption of *cimarrón*, a Spanish term for "runaway" or "wild one."

http://en.wikipedia.org/wiki/Seminole

Seneca

The Seneca are a group of indigenous people native to North America. They were the nation located farthest to the west within the Six Nations or Iroquois League in New York before the American Revolution. While exact population figures are unknown, approximately 15,000 to 25,000 Seneca live in Canada, near Brantford, Ontario, at the Six Nations of the Grand River First Nation. They are descendants of Seneca who resettled there, as they had been allies of the British during the American Revolution. Nearly 30,000 Seneca live in the United States, on and off reservations around Buffalo, New York and in Oklahoma.

http://en.wikipedia.org/wiki/Seneca_people

Shawnee

The Shawnee or Shawnee nation (Shaawanwaki, Ša·wano·ki and Shaawanowi lenaweeki) are an Algonquian-speaking people native to North America. In colonial times they were a semi-migratory Native American nation, at times inhabiting areas spanning present-day Ohio, Virginia, West Virginia, Western Maryland, South Carolina, Kentucky, Illinois, Indiana, and Pennsylvania in the United States. They were removed to Indian Territory west of the Mississippi River in the 1830s. Today the three federally recognized Shawnee tribes all headquartered in Oklahoma. The United Remnant Band of the Shawnee Nation is a state-recognized tribe based in Ohio, where it has bought some land.

http://en.wikipedia.org/wiki/Shawnee

Shoshone

The Shoshone or Shoshoni are a Native American tribe with three large divisions: Eastern Shoshone, Wyoming, northern Colorado and Montana; Northern Shoshone, eastern Idaho, western Wyoming, and northeastern Utah; and Western Shoshone, Oregon, Idaho, Utah. They traditionally speak the Shoshoni language, part of the Numic languages branch of the large Uto-Aztecan language family. The Shoshone were sometimes called the Snake Indians by neighboring tribes and early European-Americans.

http://en.wikipedia.org/wiki/Shoshone_people

Sturgeon Lake First Nation

The Sturgeon Lake First Nation is located on the eastern shores of Sturgeon Lake (Saskatchewan) about 29 km northwest of Prince Albert, Saskatchewan. The First Nation's territory consists of one Indian Reserve, Sturgeon Lake Indian Reserve No. 101. It is located in the transition zone between the aspen parkland and boreal forest biomes. The reserve borders the Rural Municipalities of Shellbrook No. 493 and Buckland No. 491, as well as the Little Red River Indian Reserve No. 106C.

http://en.wikipedia.org/wiki/Sturgeon_Lake_First_Nation

Susquehannock

The Susquehannock people, also called the Conestoga (by the English) were Iroquoian-speaking Native Americans who lived in areas adjacent to the Susquehanna River and its tributaries from the southern part of what is now New York (and the lands of the Five Nations of the Iroquois Confederacy), through the entire height of East-central and central Pennsylvania (West of the Poconos and the Delaware nations), with lands extending beyond the mouth of the Susquehanna in Maryland along the West bank of the Potomac at the north end of the Chesapeake Bay.

http://en.wikipedia.org/wiki/Conestoga_(people)

Sweetgrass

The Sweetgrass First Nation is a First Nation in Saskatchewan, Canada. Their territory is located 35 kilometers west of Battleford, Saskatchewan. The reserve was established as part of Treaty 6. The Nation is led by Chief Lori Whitecalf. Registered population 1751.

http://en.wikipedia.org/wiki/Sweetgrass_First_Nation

Teton - see **Lakota**

Three Affiliated Tribes

Three Affiliated Tribes, are a Native American group comprising a union of the Mandan, Hidatsa, and Arikara peoples, whose native lands ranged across the Missouri River basin in the Dakotas. Hardship, losses from infectious disease and forced relocations brought the remnants of the peoples together in the late 19th century. Today, the nation is based at the Fort Berthold Reservation in North Dakota. The Tribe consists of about 13,000 enrolled members. Nearly 4,500 live on the reservation; others live and work elsewhere.

http://en.wikipedia.org/wiki/Mandan,_Hidatsa,_and_Arikara_Nation

Tsleil-Waututh

The Tsleil-Waututh Nation, formerly known as the Burrard Indian Band or Burrard Band, is a First Nations government in the Canadian Province of British Columbia. The Tsleil-Waututh are Coast Salish people who speak the Downriver dialect of the Halkomelem language, and are closely related to but politically separate from the nearby Nation of the Skwxwúmesh (Squamish) and Musqueam

First Nations. The Tsleil-waututh Nation is a member government of the Naut'samawt Tribal Council, which includes other governments on the upper Sunshine Coast, southeastern Vancouver Island and the Tsawwassen band on the other side of the Vancouver metropolis from the Tsleil-waututh.

http://en.wikipedia.org/wiki/Tsleil-Waututh_First_Nation

Tuscarora

The Tuscarora ("hemp gatherers") are a Native American people of the Iroquoian-language family, with members in New York, Canada, and North Carolina. They coalesced as a people around the Great Lakes, likely about the same time as the rise of the five nations of the historic Iroquois tribes, based in present-day New York. Well before the arrival of Europeans in North America, the Tuscarora had migrated south and settled in the region now known as Eastern Carolina. The most numerous indigenous people in the area, they lived along the Roanoke, Neuse, Tar (*Torhunta* or *Narhontes*), and Pamlicorivers in North Carolina. They first encountered European explorers and settlers in North Carolina and Virginia.

http://en.wikipedia.org/wiki/Tuscarora_people

Umpqua

Umpqua refers to any of several distinct groups of Native Americans that live in present-day south central Oregon in the United States. The Upper Umpqua tribe is represented as the Cow Creek Band of Umpqua Tribe of Indians. The tribe signed a treaty with the U.S. federal government on September 19, 1853. The Upper Umpqua was the first Oregon tribe to sign a federal treaty. The Cow Creek Band spoke the now-extinct Takelma language. The Cow Creek Band has a reservation near the modern-day city of

Roseburg, Oregon. The Lower Umpqua tribe is represented in modern times as one of the three Confederated Tribes of Coos, Lower Umpqua and Siuslaw Indians located on the southwest Oregon Pacific coast in the United States. They spoke a language close to Siuslaw.

http://en.wikipedia.org/wiki/Umpqua_people

Ute

Ute people are an indigenous people of the Great Basin, now living primarily in Utah and Colorado. There are three Ute tribal reservations: Uintah-Ouray in northeastern Utah (3,500 members); Southern Ute in Colorado (1,500 members); and Ute Mountain which primarily lies in Colorado, but extends to Utah and New Mexico (2,000 members). The name of the state of Utah was derived from the name *Ute*. The word *Ute* means "Land of the sun" in their language. "Ute" possibly derived from the Western Apache word "yudah", meaning "high up". This has led to the misconception that "Ute" means people high up or mountain people.

http://en.wikipedia.org/wiki/Ute_people

Winnebago - see Ho-Chunk

Wyandot

The Wyandot people or Wendat, also called Huron, are indigenous peoples of North America. They traditionally spoke Wendat, an Iroquoian language. By the 15th century, the pre-contact Wyandots settled in the area of the north shore of present-day Lake Ontario, before migrating to Georgian Bay. It was in that later location that they first encountered the French explorer Samuel de Champlain in 1615. Today the Wyandot have a reserve in Quebec, Canada. In addition, they have three major settlements, two of which have independently governed, federally recognized tribes, in the United States. Due to differing development of the groups, they speak distinct forms of Wendat and Wyandot languages.

http://en.wikipedia.org/wiki/Wyandot_people

Yurok

The Yurok, whose name means "downriver people" in the neighboring Karuk language (also called *yuh'ára*, or *yurúkvaarar* in Karuk), are Native Americans who live in northwestern California near the Klamath River and Pacific coast. Their autonym is Olekwo'l meaning "Persons." Today they live on the Yurok Indian Reservation, on several rancherias, including the Trinidad Rancheria, throughout Humboldt County. They are enrolled in seven different federally recognized tribes today.

http://en.wikipedia.org/wiki/Yurok

Zuni

The Zuni (Zuni: *A:shiwi*; formerly spelled *Zuñi*) are a federally recognized Native American tribe, one of the Pueblo peoples. Most live in the Pueblo of Zuni on the Zuni River, a tributary of the Little Colorado River, in western New Mexico, United States. Zuni is 55 km (34 mi) south of Gallup, New Mexico. In addition to the reservation, the tribe owns trust lands in Catron County, New Mexico and Apache County, Arizona. They called their homeland Shiwinnaqin.

http://en.wikipedia.org/wiki/Zuni_people

ABOUT THE AUTHORS

About John

John Girard is an author, storyteller, and adventurer. He is a sought-after international speaker who is well known for his dynamic, entertaining, and informative style. He has spoken to groups on every continent (well, except for Antarctica). As a tenured full professor at Minot State University, John teaches graduate and undergraduate business classes. Engaging with students on a daily basis ensures he remains current in the ever-changing world in which we live and do business. John has traveled to more than 75 countries investigating globalization in action. A diehard fan of the millennium generation, he has traveled with college students to 22 countries witnessing their transformation to global citizens.

John has published five other books: *Tips for Two*, *Building Organizational Memories*, *A Leader's Guide to Knowledge Management*, *Social Knowledge* and *Business Goes Virtual*. His current research interests include knowledge management, social media, and globalization. John is founder and Chief Knowledge Strategist of Sagology (www.sagology.com), a firm dedicated to connecting people with people to facilitate collaboration, learning, and knowledge-sharing through keynotes, workshops, and consulting. Prior to joining the faculty at Minot State University in 2004, John worked as the Director of Knowledge Management at National Defence Headquarters in Ottawa, Canada. To learn more about John, visit www.johngirard.net

About JoAnn

JoAnn Girard is the co-founder and managing partner of Sagology, a firm that focuses on connecting people with people to collaborate and share knowledge. She has worked on a variety of knowledge-intensive research projects, which considered issues such as information anxiety, enterprise dementia, and organizational memories. An avid traveler, JoAnn has visited more than 70 countries.

JoAnn has published four other books: *Tips for Two*, *A Leader's Guide to Knowledge Management*, *Social Knowledge* and *Business Goes Virtual*. Prior to forming Sagology, JoAnn was cofounder of two successful technology companies. Yachtclub.net developed and hosted web presences for yachting companies in the USA, England, Scotland, Spain, Gibraltar, and Greece. Quid Pro Quo Software developed educational and edutainment software, including their flagship game, Trivia Mania. Before entering the high-tech arena, JoAnn worked in the travel industry and as a school librarian. The experience she gained in these information-intensive positions proved especially valuable as she considers the knowledge challenges confronting executives today.

JoAnn dedicates most of her spare time to animals. She is a board member of her local zoological society and volunteers as an interpretive speaker at the zoo.

INDEX

Bold entries are clan titles from section two.

A

Abenaki, 88
ability, 38
abundant, 36
abused, 67
accorded, 39
accordingly, 65
action, 36, 85
afraid, 5, 7, 55, 84
aged, 46
agreed, 55
alone, 7, 20, 35, 57, 68, 81
amauti, 68
American, i, 76
ancestors, 31
anchor, 21
angry, 74
animal, 3, 20, 50, 66
Anishinaabe, 88
answer, 45
answered, 75
answers, 13
ant, 63
Apache, 88
Arapaho, 89
arguing, 42, 65
Arikara, 89
arrow, 7
arrows, 54, 73
ashamed, 36, 38
asked, 26, 71
asleep, 16, 39
Assiniboine, 89
assist, 25
assume, 65
attack, 57
autumn, 56, 60
ax, 28

B

babes, 26

backward, 56
bad, 45, 66
bark, 52, 57
barking, 62
beach, 57, 68
beads, 54
bear, 25
bears, 83
beast, 8
beautiful, 16, 57, 75
beauty, 3, 16, 40, 44, 47, 52, 65, 67
become, 42, 76
beliefs, 47
believe, 6, 52, 56, 78
believes, 42
belongings, 32
beneficial, 21
big, 68
birds, 17, 18, 48, 50, 80
birth, 9
Blackfoot, 90
blankets, 49
blessings, 19, 34, 83
blizzard, 36
blood, 6, 19, 31, 76, 83
bloom, 17
blue, 50
boat, 15, 70
boats, 15
body, 32, 34
bond, 12
books, 18
boring, 50
born, 48, 56, 59, 66
borrow, 33, 72
borrowed, 12
bottle, 37
bowl, 44
bowls, 44
boy, 3, 25
brave, 18, 36, 37, 78
braveness, 78
breath, 8, 20, 40, 73
breeds, 60
broken, 47, 50
buffalo, 66, 73
build, 43
buildings, 48
burdens, 25

C

calm, 17
canoe, 15, 70
carefully, 22
caribou, 33
catch, 23, 63
cats, 22
caught, 3, 62
cease, 56, 60
celebration, 79
center, 41, 49, 66
ceremonies, 19
chain, 20
chair, 79
changes, 33
check, 15
Cherokee, 58, 90
Cheyenne, 91
chiefs, 24, 49
child, 9, 33, 42
childhood, 6, 27
children, 10, 14, 26, 31, 33,

SAGE SAYINGS

34, 37, 38, 48, 52, 58, 68, 70, 72, 75, 84
Chippewa, 91
Chiricahua, 91
choose, 52, 54
churches, 7
circle, 6, 14, 19
civilization, 48
clean, 72
close, 3
clothes, 15
clouds, 57
cold, 15, 65
color, 11, 45
Comanche, 92
comfort, 3
common, 43
community, 44, 78
company, 17
concealed, 59
concern, 17
concrete, 48
Conestoga, 92
connect, 71
conquered, 18
conscience, 31
consider, 43
consists, 32
constant, 41
contains, 21
contaminate, 66
contented, 56
control, 55
cooked, 12
cooking, 61
cornerstone, 39
council, 58

counselor, 52
country, 10, 68
courtesy, 28
coward, 31, 78
create, 44
creates, 4
cried, 59
Crow, 92
crows, 64, 84
cry, 5, 22, 38, 77, 84
culture, 30, 83
cure, 25
curiosity, 4
cut, 3, 18, 62

D

Dakota, 93
dance, 18
danger, 32, 56, 73
dangerous, 46, 65
dark, 6, 22, 44
darkens, 20
darkness, 74
daughter, 25
days, 29, 71
dead, 82
deaf, 13, 52
death, 5, 14, 29, 33, 45, 48, 51, 66, 81
debt, 10
deceitful, 29
decisions, 32, 43
deepest, 50
defeated, 36
Delaware, 93
delay, 26

deliberation, 43
demand, 47
denied, 56
depend, 72
desire, 77
destination, 39
destiny, 44
destroy, 57
destroyed, 36
did, 10
die, 4, 14, 48, 59, 68, 81
died, 57
dies, 78
differ, 55
difference, 5, 44, 45
difficult, 46
disappear, 5
discover, 18
discovered, 10, 83
disease, 25
dishonest, 77
disrespect, 60
distance, 18, 37, 78
divide, 14
divine, 49
dog, 52, 57
dogs, 26, 29, 62
done, 44, 71, 79
door, 35
dove, 83
dream, 67, 77
dreamed, 77
dreams, 16, 84
drink, 36, 58
drinking, 48
drumbeat, 44
due, 56

Duwamish, 93
dying, 16

E

eager, 79
eagle, 13, 50
eagles, 84
early, 40
earth, 6, 7, 8, 9, 25, 27, 30, 31, 33, 34, 61, 65
easy, 18, 37, 78
eat, 3, 18, 23, 62
eaten, 20, 62
either, 61
elder, 41
elders, 14, 58, 76, 79, 81, 83
eloquent, 59
emerge, 74
encounter, 83
ended, 65
enemy, 21, 36
enjoy, 57
enough, 72, 77, 83
enter, 33, 34, 41
entirely, 32
envious, 63
environment, 48
equal, 23, 57
even, 70, 80, 82
evenly, 23
eventually, 66
ever, 17, 20, 35
everlasting, 76
everywhere, 26, 35, 66
evil, 4, 17
exactly, 80

existence, 17, 25, 28
expect, 56
experiences, 82
explains, 49
expressed, 70
eye, 27, 63, 80
eyes, 10, 21, 29, 31, 40, 44, 47, 50, 53, 82

F

face, 3, 81
faces, 84
fact, 32
faith, 44, 56, 71
fall, 70
fallen, 37
falls, 6
family, 24, 64
far, 9
farther, 82
father, 46
fathers, 54
fault, 26
faults, 59
fear, 33, 34, 48, 55, 71, 81, 83
feeling, 26
feet, 35
fellow, 48
fellows, 41
felt, 71
fences, 74
few, 76
fiercely, 25
fight, 25, 62
fighting, 21

fill, 17
filled, 48, 52, 81
finger, 66
finished, 18
fire, 47, 50, 58, 61
firefly, 73
fish, 3, 48, 62
flash, 73
fleas, 29
flourish, 35
fly, 20
focused, 36
following, 66
food, 32, 40, 43
foolish, 62
foot, 70
footprints, 7, 46
forefathers, 72
foreseen, 56
forests, 48
forever, 67, 81
forget, 24
forgotten, 17
fortunate, 53
found, 27, 31, 47
fox, 13
free, 5, 7, 54, 56, 84
freely, 25
friend, 14, 16, 23, 69
friends, 25, 27
friendship, 20, 22, 25, 53
frog, 36
front, 78
fruitful, 75, 80
full, 16
fun, 72
future, 11, 17, 26, 31, 47, 54,

guilty, 64

G

gain, 61
garden, 56
gather, 64
generations, 43
generosity, 38, 40, 81
gentleness, 38
gift, 27, 49, 69, 70, 74, 85
gifts, 6
given, 20, 33, 72
giver, 49
glorious, 34
glory, 56, 60
goods, 76
got, 49
grain, 81
grandchildren, 34, 48
grandfather, 45
grandfathers, 78
grandmothers, 44
grasses, 84
grateful, 39, 42
great, 11, 14, 19, 23, 32, 42, 50, 52, 64, 72, 81
greater, 24
grew, 71
grieved, 40
grovel, 22
grow, 9, 22, 35
growing, 16
guard, 79
guest, 65
guidance, 83
guide, 44

H

had, 10, 47, 82
hair, 33
half-avoided, 56
handed, 72
handsome, 58
happen, 64, 69, 85
happened, 55
happiness, 21, 82
happy, 24, 41
harmless, 83
harmony, 30, 31
hate, 28
heal, 44
healing, 82
heart, 9, 13, 14, 16, 17, 22, 26, 27, 30, 33, 34, 35, 39, 41, 42, 47, 50, 63, 75, 76, 82
hearts, 4, 6, 18, 19, 32, 48, 49, 55, 70, 72, 75, 81, 82
heirloom, 59
held, 52
help, 31, 42
helping, 24
herb, 25
heritage, 28
hero, 48, 81
history, 66
Ho-Chunk, 94
hold, 51
holiness, 79
home, 48, 66, 68, 81
homes, 84

honesty, 81
honor, 46, 67
honorable, 5, 42
hope, 46, 83
Hopi, 94
host, 28
house, 41, 49
hovers, 16
hug, 65
humanity, 21
humble, 51
humility, 28, 60, 65
hundred, 20
hungry, 20, 54, 65, 70
hunted, 18
hunting, 15, 23
Huron, 94
hurt, 58

I

ice, 55
igloo, 43
ignorance, 16
ignore, 71
immersed, 16
impact, 43
important, 3, 51, 71
impurity, 12
independent, 29, 80
Indians, 10, 46, 49
individuality, 80
inhabit, 76
inherit, 33
intended, 80
intrudes, 30
intuition, 34

Inuit, 94
involved, 32
Iroquois, 95
itchy, 33

J

jealous, 36
job, 44
journey, 9, 14
joy, 35, 43, 53, 73
judge, 4, 12, 50, 63
jumps, 13
justified, 65

K

keepers, 68
keeps, 24
kind, 79
kindle, 58
kindled, 58
kindness, 69, 70, 76
Kiowa, 96
knife, 74
know, 25, 55, 76
knowing, 34, 71
knowledge, 11, 26, 61, 69, 74
known, 35, 67, 70, 75
knows, 50, 57, 59

L

labor, 26, 58, 61
lacks, 44
Lakota, 96

lame, 13
lamented, 55
land, 3, 19, 20, 47, 76, 78, 83
lands, 76
language, 11, 25, 28, 30, 48
languages, 8
large, 49
late, 24
law, 33, 54
laws, 33, 43
lazy, 63, 71
lead, 54, 78
leader, 12, 13, 14, 15, 53
leadership, 26, 51, 77
leaf, 17
learn, 8, 12, 40, 48, 75, 79
learned, 48, 79
learning, 10
least, 72
leaves, 18
leaving, 28
led, 15
Lenape, 97
lengthy, 26
lent, 37
leopards, 22
levels, 28
liar, 48
liberty, 56
library, 3, 18
lids, 80
lie, 12, 16, 29
lies, 26, 32, 54
life, 6, 8, 15, 20, 23, 27, 33, 35, 44, 51, 53, 58, 59, 71, 73, 80
lift, 64, 66

light, 40, 42
lightning, 60
lights, 24
limited, 38
lips, 84
liquor, 58
listen, 8, 31, 34, 41, 60, 62, 68
lit, 58
living, 8, 11, 21, 30, 43, 58, 80, 82
loaned, 33
lone, 10
longest, 14
looked, 21
looking, 3, 4, 80
lost, 44, 71
love, 5, 6, 8, 11, 12, 14, 24, 34, 55, 65, 68, 72, 74, 76, 81
loved, 83
loves, 6, 64
lower, 42
luck, 66
Lumbee, 97
lying, 29

M

mainly, 30
manner, 79
Maricopa, 97
mark, 64, 69, 73
married, 43, 51
mature, 45
meaning, 8, 60
means, 71

measure, 48
meat, 9, 47, 61
memories, 46
memory, 67
minds, 31
mine, 40
Miniconjou, 98
Minquass, 98
minute, 15
miracle, 27
misinterpretations, 32
mission, 25
mist, 6
misunderstandings, 32
moccasin, 7, 59
moccasins, 4, 12
Mohawk, 98
Mohican, 99
moment, 82
money, 3, 18, 49, 62
monster, 68
moon, 16, 62
moons, 4, 12
morning, 7, 43
most, 5, 21
mother, 9, 23
mothers, 44
mountain, 63, 81
mountains, 27
mouse, 12
mouth, 60
moved, 53
moves, 9
moving, 80
Muskoday, 99
mysteries, 43
mystery, 23

myth, 13

N

naked, 68
name, 5
nation, 18, 68
nations, 35, 58, 69
nature, 9, 21, 31, 70, 72, 75
Navajo, 99, 100
needed, 50
needs, 7, 57, 59
negative, 62
neighbor, 4, 28, 52
new, 7, 44, 82
next, 43
night, 73
noble, 14, 26, 77
noose, 60
nourish, 9
nourishes, 29
Nuxalk, 100

O

obedience, 12
obey, 54
offend, 28
offended, 29
Oglala Lakota, 101
Ojibwe, 101
old, 13, 14, 16, 52, 63, 71
older, 79
Omaha, 102
once, 73, 78
Oneida, 102
oneness, 66

ones, 30, 76, 82
oneself, 50
ongoing, 37
Onondaga, 103
opened, 6
opinion, 25
Osage, 103
outside, 36, 53, 85
overcome, 11
overly, 83

P

paid, 78
pain, 42
Paiute, 104
pale, 44
parents, 30, 33
party, 23
pass, 27
passing, 34
past, 11, 17, 40, 54, 55
path, 22, 35, 52
paths, 45
patience, 56
patiently, 69
Pawnee, 104
pay, 21
peace, 6, 19, 24, 31, 35, 44, 49, 68, 69, 75, 77, 80, 85
peaceably, 5, 19
peaceful, 36, 83
peacefully, 83
pebble, 66
penalty, 54
penned, 56
perfect, 12

perfection, 19
performed, 70
pick, 28
Pima, 104
pipe, 74
pitying, 57
place, 14, 26, 41, 49, 82
placed, 80
Plains, 105
plants, 34, 60
play, 24, 57, 68
pleases, 56
pleasures, 63
point, 54
poison, 67
poisoned, 3, 62
polar, 83
political, 82
polluted, 18
Ponca, 105
pond, 36
possess, 42
possessions, 11
possible, 51
pot, 12
Potawatomi, 106
power, 8, 14, 19, 22, 32, 60, 61
powers, 66, 80
pray, 20, 48, 81
prayer, 28, 54
pregnant, 63
presence, 23
present, 17, 28, 62, 64
preserves, 17
pretending, 16, 39
prevent, 64

prevented, 40
price, 61
pride, 28
prize, 21
problem, 77
problems, 82
proclaimed, 75
promises, 47
pronounce, 53
proper, 64
properly, 11
property, 61
protect, 48, 57, 59
protecting, 54
protection, 15
Pueblo, 106
pursue, 63

Q

quarrel, 7, 72
quickly, 26, 64, 79
quietly, 5, 16, 31

R

rabbit, 13
rain, 6
rainbow, 6, 10, 53, 82
raised, 26
rather, 48
rattlesnakes, 59
reach, 79
read, 50, 55
ready, 25
really, 3, 44, 66
reason, 26, 42, 80

rebuild, 49
receive, 13, 58, 76
received, 65
red, 45, 68
regarding, 47
regards, 46
rejoice, 59
rejoiced, 59
relate, 48
related, 4
relationship, 66
relatives, 8, 11, 61
relearn, 38
released, 73
religion, 47, 54, 55, 57, 72, 85
religions, 39
rely, 80
remain, 33
remains, 67
remember, 24, 31, 38, 47, 78
reminded, 77
reminds, 16
remove, 74
render, 77
rent, 21
replace, 10
represent, 31
require, 37
resides, 26
resistance, 59
resource, 59
respect, 8, 10, 22, 30, 47, 53, 55, 61, 71, 76
respectful, 27
respond, 30
responsibility, 22, 68, 73

results, 65
returned, 70
returns, 29
rhythm, 44
rich, 11, 64
rifle, 72
right, 11, 14, 25, 46, 47, 68, 82
rights, 23
river, 3, 15, 39, 62, 70, 74
rivers, 56, 74
road, 14
rocked, 26
rocky, 28
room, 79
root, 9, 17
rooted, 3
rules, 71
run, 56, 81
running, 10
runs, 73

S

sacred, 17, 31, 38, 79, 81
sad, 7
safe, 18, 78
salute, 40
sand, 81
Santee, 107
satisfied, 7
Sauk, 107
saved, 6
saw, 49
saying, 62
says, 57
scatter, 64

scout, 46
screams, 10
sea, 68
season, 55
secrets, 43
seed, 74
seeking, 13
seeks, 50
seems, 9
seen, 72
selected, 46
selfhood, 17
self-loving, 36
sell, 20
Seminole, 107
Seneca, 108
seniors, 45
senses, 34
separate, 45
separated, 35
serpent, 83
servant, 13, 38
serve, 28, 41, 55
serves, 41
service, 26, 27, 45, 46, 77
setting, 29
severest, 52
sew, 51
shadow, 73
shallow, 63
shame, 64
shamed, 62
shared, 38
shares, 8, 20
shark, 57
Shawnee, 108
sheltered, 26

shoots, 31
shore, 14
shortly, 80
Shoshone, 108
shoulder, 41
showing, 84
siblings, 34
sick, 5, 47
sight, 29, 84
sign, 53
silent, 41
simplicity, 46
simply, 51, 72
sing, 23, 64, 82
singing, 17
single, 76
Sioux, 29, 68, 74
sister, 25
sisters, 60
sit, 45
size, 50
sky, 4, 27, 50, 53, 57, 75, 79, 80
slave, 58
sleep, 47, 61
slide, 51
slowly, 19
small, 11, 12
smart, 43, 85
smarter, 57, 59
smile, 38, 49
smooth, 11, 25
snow, 23, 55
snows, 41
soccer, 24
softly, 11, 41
soldier, 46

solution, 36, 85
solutions, 82
someday, 53
someone, 32, 42, 84
somewhere, 63
song, 14, 37, 48, 67, 81
soon, 76
sorrows, 63
soul, 7, 10, 82
speaking, 34, 58
speaks, 41, 76
spear, 68
species, 80
speech, 27
spend, 18
spider, 49
spin, 16
spinning, 33
spirit, 8, 15, 20, 33, 34, 43, 53
spirits, 76, 82
spiritual, 12, 15, 29, 82, 83
spite, 51
spoken, 4, 12
spring, 63
stain, 19, 83
stars, 4
start, 80
starts, 50
starving, 62
steady, 51
step, 82
stepping, 39
still, 17, 34
stomach, 54
stones, 18, 39
stop, 54, 80

stopped, 55
stories, 71
storm, 36
storms, 17
story, 76
straight, 7, 72
stranger, 70
strangles, 60
strength, 21, 28, 38, 54
strife, 19
strike, 73
striking, 74
string, 54
Sturgeon Lake, 109
submit, 54
successful, 77
suffer, 66
suffering, 35
suffocate, 66
sun, 7, 19, 26, 65
sunlight, 72
sunrise, 58
sunset, 58, 73
surrounded, 16
survive, 44, 56
Susquehannock, 109
sustains, 9
swallow, 33
sweet, 7, 9
Sweetgrass, 110
system, 10

T

tail, 59
taken, 49
takes, 9, 64, 76

taking, 71
talent, 79
talk, 23, 27, 47, 52, 54, 60
talking, 47, 84
tall, 48
taste, 21
tasted, 58
taught, 21
taxes, 10
teach, 7, 30, 34
teacher, 16, 39
teachers, 54
teaches, 72
tears, 10, 27, 38, 47, 82
tells, 71
temper, 16
tender, 84
test, 52
Teton, 110
thank, 40
thankful, 72
thanks, 9, 19, 21, 26, 43
theory, 25
these, ii, 34
think, 48, 54, 75, 76, 79
thinking, 57, 59, 80
thirsty, 23
thorny, 34
thousand, 76
thread, 71
threads, 49
Three Affiliated Tribes, 110
through, 19, 33, 83
throw, 51
thrust, 81
thunder, 60

times, 78
tiny, 26
tired, 47, 65
today, 18, 30, 32, 71, 85
tomorrow, 32
tongue, 13, 45, 52, 53, 76
town, 15
trade, 54
tradition, 77
traditional, 30
train, 68
travel, 54
treasures, 21, 72
treatment, 77
trees, 18, 26, 48
trembling, 53
trials, 69
trouble, 6, 47
troublemaker, 34
trust, 34, 44, 63
truth, 20, 28, 31, 37, 65, 81, 83
truthful, 27
Tsleil-Waututh, 110
Tuscarora, 111
twitching, 80, 84

U

ugly, 52
Umpqua, 111
understand, 8, 17, 24, 55
undertaking, 72
undoing, 56
unfolding, 44
unfriendly, 42
uniting, 49

unity, 12
universe, 27, 30, 45, 66
unjust, 6
unknown, 19
unless, 14
unreservedly, 39
unsafe, 18
unseen, 61
unshaken, 17
upcoming, 73
Ute, 112

V

valid, 42
valuable, 76
value, 76
victim, 73
village, 9
vineyard, 28
virtue, 5
vision, 23, 50
voice, 21, 22, 72

W

wait, 69
waiting, 70, 76
wake, 16, 39
waking, 84
walk, 4, 5, 11, 13, 14, 16, 20, 78, 82
walked, 12
walking, 30
walks, 5, 13
wander, 51
wanted, 35

warm, 48
warmed, 26
warning, 73
warriors, 18, 44
wash, 64
waste, 66
watch, 18, 52
water, 48, 55, 58
waters, 18, 27
ways, 17, 40
weak, 38
weakness, 11, 21
weapons, 18
wear, 15
weather, 15, 69
web, 16, 71
webs, 49
weep, 7, 48, 81
welfare, 58
whispers, 10
whistle, 24
whit, 81
whole, 9, 16, 40
whom, 46
wicked, 68
wife, 26
willing, 15
wind, 53, 66
winds, 26
wing, 50
Winnebago, 112
winter, 56, 60
wintertime, 73
wisdom, 11, 13, 26, 61, 68

wise, 43, 83, 85
wiser, 50, 84
wisest, 82, 85
wish, 5, 19, 57, 83, 84
wishes, 5
wolf, 10, 62
woman, 84
women, 10, 18
won, 10
wonder, 69, 74, 85
work, 10, 54
world, 3, 5, 13, 16, 18, 44, 59, 61, 68, 71
worlds, 51
worldview, 30
worn, 76
worship, 55
wounded, 66
woven, 71
wrong, 11, 25, 28, 71
wrongdoers, 64
wrongdoing, 64
Wyandot, 112

Y

years, 58
yesterday, 18, 30, 85
youth, 16, 45, 63
Yurok, 113

Z

Zuni, 113